STARS
in Her Heart

STARS
in Her Heart

ELLA M. ROBINSON

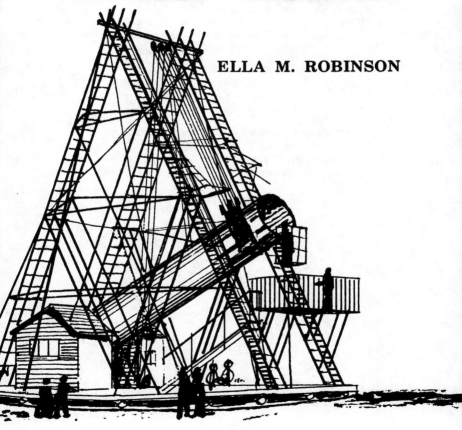

TEACH Services, Inc.
New York

2005   06 07 08 09 10 11 12   ·5 4 3 2 1

Copyright © 2005 TEACH Services, Inc.
ISBN-13: 978-1-57258-318-5
ISBN-10: 1-57258-318-5
Library of Congress Catalog Card No. 2004118387

Published by
TEACH Services, Inc.
www.TEACHServices.com

Contents

Chapter 1

Little Sister

ONE SUNDAY morning Frau Anna Herschel led her three-year-old daughter, Caroline Lucretia, down the long aisle of the garrison church to a seat in the front. Bending over the little girl, she whispered, "Dort ist dein bruder Jakob! ["There is your brother Jacob!"] He is playing the big new organ."

In another instant Jacob opened up with a grand prelude. The music rolled out with such a loud, booming sound that the child took fright. Before her mother could close the gate of their pew, Caroline dashed down the aisle and out the door, and she ran all the way home as fast as her trembling legs would take her.

Mother followed behind, calling, "Wait! Wait! Caroline! Wait for mamma!" In time the little girl learned to enjoy the grand, melodious music that filled the church whenever her nineteen-year-old brother took his place at the organ.

This was in an army garrison in the city of Hanover, Germany, more than two hundred years ago.

But while Caroline loved her oldest brother, it was her second brother, William, that she really adored. Someday she would make William famous. Kings and princes would come to visit him, and this great fame would be largely a result of Caroline's work. But right now all that was in the future. Caroline was a little girl, and William was fourteen.

Caroline always remembered the solemn service when William was confirmed, that is, received as a full member in the Lutheran Church. That very month he had been admitted to the regimental band of the Hanoverian foot guards, of which his father and Jacob were members. In wartime the foot guards marched with the fighting men, beating drums and blowing wind instruments to bolster the morale of the soldiers. In peacetime they joined the court orchestra in entertaining officials of state and conducting concerts.

On this particular Sunday morning, as William stood up in the front of the church with the other teen-agers who were to make their vows and receive the blessing from the solemn, kindly bishop, he wore his new band uniform. Caroline's heart swelled with pride. "William is the handsomest and the smartest of them all," she said to herself. "I have the most wonderful brother in all the world."

Soon after that, Caroline's sister, Sophia, was married. In the stories that Caroline wrote about her life she told about the wedding. "Sophia had been away from home," she wrote. "I had never seen her until the day she returned to be married to Griesbach, one of the musicians in the band. The

8

newlyweds were to occupy a part of the house in which we lived.

"Following the wedding there was a feast and dance, with plenty of gay music furnished by the band. I was three and a half years old, and I joined the merriment, whirling round and round, trying to keep out from underfoot, all the while imagining that I was having a wonderfully good time, even without a partner."

Father Herschel was a musician by profession. He earned a small salary by playing the oboe in the band and by teaching stringed instruments. He taught all his sons to play the violin, the oboe, and the guitar. He even made the instruments on which they began their lessons.

Frequently there were private concerts in their home or the homes of neighbors. Caroline wrote: "After such an entertainment my father and brothers would sometimes sit up late into the night, discussing the evening's program, and criticizing, for their own improvement, the various musical performances. Jacob was the best player of the three boys.

" 'I think music the most worth while of all accomplishments,' he would say. 'To me it seems the only thing worth spending time on.'

"But William thought that there were other kinds of learning, such as science, mathematics, and philosophy, that were just as important as music. Before the evening's conversation was far advanced he would be leading out in a discussion of the latest discoveries in physics, chemistry, natural science, or astronomy. When the names of Leibnitz, Newton, and Euler resounded too loud, mamma would appear: 'Come, come, boys! It is nearly midnight! You know the little ones have to be in school by seven in the morning.' "

Even William's mother did not realize how important all this talk would be. She did not know that her young son would grow up to be one of the world's greatest astronomers.

Even after the boys had gone, very reluctantly, to their room, they would continue talking, until Jacob and Alexander would fall asleep. William, discovering that he had no audience, would finally quiet down. On such occasions, three-year-old Caroline would try to keep herself awake as long as possible, for, as she wrote later, "though I understood little of what was said, yet it made me happy to see them so happy."

One day when Caroline was not quite four years old, she was told that she could start going to school. Alexander, her eight-year-old brother, had been attending for several years. His father solemnly commissioned him to take good care of his little sister at school. As soon as breakfast was over, the two set off together, little Caroline laughing and chattering happily as she trudged along by the side of her "big, big brother."

Sophia, Caroline's married sister, was not well. Although she loved her brothers and sisters, the noise of so many children in one little house made her nervous. So in the afternoons when school was out, their mother would call, "Come, Alex, you and Caroline go outside and play." This was not too bad in the summertime when there were neighbor children around to join them in lively games, or even in the winter when there were snow forts to build and snow battles to fight. But often Alexander would run off to skate on the ice in the town ditch, leaving Caroline to trudge along the bank, or to stand half freezing and watch the others until her brother was ready to return home. Tearfully she would say to herself, "There's nobody who cares anything about me. I wish somebody loved me."

One day when Caroline was five years old she was with her mother in the bedroom, when suddenly the floor began to move. She dropped the shoe she was putting on. Her mother grabbed hold of the bedstead with one hand and her little girl with the other. Her brothers came running into the room, Sophia following them. The shaking continued for several minutes, while everyone in the room stood panic-stricken, wondering what was going to happen to them next. This was the morning of November 1, 1755, when the famous earthquake and tidal wave killed thousands of people in the city of Lisbon, Portugal, twelve hundred miles to the west.

Soon after this, trouble broke out between England and France, and Caroline's father and two older brothers had to go with the regimental band to England. (During all the years of this story, the rulers of Hanover were also the kings of England. George II—as well as George III after him—was king of England and of the American colonies, and at the same time ruler of his home territory of Hanover in Germany. Several times during these years England was at war with France.) By 1756 Caroline's father had spent eight years in foreign service as a member of the band, coming home only for occasional visits. As a result of exposure to wet and cold, he always suffered from asthma and rheumatism.

Now after nine years of quiet, England was threatened by an invasion of the French, and the Hanoverian guards were ordered across the channel to England to replace English troops that had been sent abroad. Although he was in poor health, father was obliged to march away with the guards' band, Jacob and William with him. Caroline wrote:

"My dear father was thin and pale; also my brother William was of delicate constitution. The whole town was in motion, with drums beating and soldiers hallooing and shouting in the streets. Griesbach came to join my father and brothers, and in a moment they were all gone. Sophia fled to her room. Alexander followed along behind the troops to take a last look. I found myself with my mother in a room all in confusion. Our tears were flowing. Neither of us could speak. I snatched a large handkerchief of my father's from a chair, picked up a stool, and placed it at my mother's feet. I sat down on the stool, put one corner of the handkerchief into her hand, and held the opposite corner myself. Mother gave me a wan smile, and then we wept together. I was five years old. My new little brother, Dietrich, lay in his cradle in a corner of the room. Sophia moved in to live with us. We had a lonely time."

But in less than a year the troops were back again. The expected invasion of England had not taken place. While in camp, William had improved his time in study and had learned, among other things, to speak and write English. Caroline wrote about his homecoming:

"My mother, being very busy preparing the dinner, had allowed me to go to the parade ground to meet my father. But I could not find him anywhere, nor anyone else whom I knew. So, when nearly frozen to death, I came home and found them all at the table. They were so happy at seeing one another that, at first, no one noticed me. I stood there feeling very lonely and nearly ready to cry.

"But my brother William, glancing up, quickly laid down his knife and fork and ran forward to greet me. He kneeled down at my feet as he would kneel to a princess, and taking my cold little hand in his big warm one, pressed it to his lips and said, 'How happy I am to see my little Lina again!' Immediately I forgot all my grievances. William had noticed me! He cared about me! He was *the best and dearest of brothers.* I was happy."

After a few quiet months at home the Hanoverian guards were again called into action, and in the early spring of 1757 father and the two older brothers went with their regiment.

After the men marched away to war, sadness settled down on Hanover, and it grew deeper every day as reports continued to arrive of defeats of the Hanoverian and British troops by the invaders.

The troops suffered greatly in the campaign. After long and tiring marches they were often forced to camp in plowed fields where the furrows were filled with water from heavy rains. William was weak and pale, and his father feared that he did not have the strength to continue with the guards during wartime.

One day, while camped within gunshot of a fierce battle at Hastenbeck, he said, "Son, I think you should consider your own safety and return to Hanover."

William was eighteen. He took his father's advice, for he had no military ambitions and was glad to get away. Although England was the land of his dreams, yet he had many friends among the French and was not eager to fight them. But when he reached home, after a tramp of twenty miles, his mother was alarmed.

"You must return to the camp at once," she insisted. "Go back to your father and join the guards' band again."

When William got back to the army, he found that in the confusion following the defeat at Hastenbeck, nobody had time to look after the musicians or to tell them what to do. The musicians did not seem to be needed. After a period of enforced idleness William made his way to Hamburg, where he was joined by his brother, Jacob, who was in the same plight as himself. Together they crossed over to England.

Alexander and his little sister continued to attend the day school at the garrison. Classes were held till three o'clock in the afternoon. After school each day Caroline would go to another school to learn knitting, before returning home.

Although she was only seven years old Caroline completed her training in the school of knitting and took up the never-ending task of providing the family with stockings. She must have been very small, for she tells that when she stood up to finish the first stocking she made, it reached the floor! She gave the finished pair to Alexander.

After the disastrous battle of Hastenbeck the Hanoverians were not allowed to return to their homes. They were interned in a camp near the scene of their defeat.

During the French occupation, which lasted nearly two years, the Hanoverians were compelled to care for the victorious soldiers. Nearly every house in the city was jammed. From fourteen to sixteen privates and officers were crowded into the house occupied by the Herschels. Many of the forests had been destroyed, making firewood hard to get. Food was scarce. Sophia and her mother were often in tears.

Caroline was miserable. It didn't seem like home with her father and two big brothers gone and the house full of strangers. She hated to be snubbed and ignored. Mother worked so hard and was so tired that she could hardly keep from scolding when Caroline did not finish her tasks, and it seemed to the little girl that she never could get through them all.

Often she would cry when her big sister was cross with her. But in the next minute she would brush away the tears and try to smile as she washed dishes and scoured pots and helped her mother cook the food and wait on the soldiers. She discovered that tears made no contribution to the sum total of happiness, but that smiling and singing and helping were the best kind of medicine to drive away the blues.

One day she said, "Mother, I can write your letters to father if you will tell me what to write." Soldiers' wives looked in and saw the little girl with pen and paper. After that, the seven-year-old girl was the official letter writer for the neighborhood, for many of the women could not write.

The distressing conditions in Hanover continued for more than a year, until Prince Ferdinand of Brunswick was sent with fresh troops to relieve the Hanoverian army and succeeded in driving the French back. Roads were bad and progress was slow, but by July the encampment had moved to within a few miles of the city and the soldiers' wives could visit them.

Father Herschel was so crippled by rheumatism and weakened by loss of sleep due to his asthma that he had to resign his position in the band, but he set about to earn what he could giving lessons and copying music. Printed music was scarce, and the copies used by teachers and music conductors had to be made by hand. When his asthma kept him awake, he would sit up half the night copying, and Caroline would read to him to keep him company while he worked.

Jacob returned from England. How Caroline wished it might have been William! William was always kind, but Jacob bullied her. He would scold, "You stupid, awkward child! Always spilling things! When will you learn to wait on the table properly?" This made her all the more nervous and clumsy.

The first thing Father Herschel did on his arrival from camp was to take the little homemade violin from its place on the shelf, restring it, and give Caroline's little brother, Dietrich, a lesson. After that, no matter how busy father was with other pupils, Dietrich had his music lesson every day. Before he was five years old he played his small violin at a public concert, standing on a table like the boy Mozart. The audience applauded loudly, and he was praised and caressed. One lady even slipped a gold coin into his pocket.

Caroline wrote: "I was proud of my cute, sprightly little brother, and was pleased when he was praised and petted, for I loved him. But, oh, how I wished that I too might learn to play! Whenever I heard father call, 'Come, son! come for your lesson!' I would quickly snatch up my knitting and follow him.

"Then I would sit in a corner of the room, and while my needles clicked, I would listen to father give the lesson. I was determined to learn as much as possible for myself. Once in a while after my little brother had finished his practicing, before the violin was laid aside, father would teach me a new piece of music or help me master some difficult

trick on the instrument. He always seemed pleased to help me, and I am sure he would have given me regular lessons had it not been for mother. But she had decided opinions of her own about the kind of education that would make her daughter useful. She would say, 'Little girls must learn to work. They must learn to do the common, everyday tasks about the home. I am not going to have you ruined with too much book learning and music and all those fine things.'

"So for the sake of peace in the family, whatever help I received with my music was usually given on the quiet, when mother was away from home or too much occupied with her housework to notice what was going on in the music room."

By dint of perseverance, Caroline was able, at the age of ten, to join the other players in the orchestra as second violinist. A happier little girl there never was—until one morning when she woke up and tried to dress herself and found she was too weak to stand on her feet. She could not eat, and was so nauseated and felt so sick all over that she flung herself back into the bed, where she lay for many days tossing with fever. No one held any hope for her life except her mother. She watched over her sick child anxiously, but even she feared that every day would be her last. "Typhus," said the doctor.

After two weeks Caroline began to mend, very slowly at first. For a long time she was so weak that she had to crawl up and down stairs on her hands and knees. She was eleven years old at the time of her illness, and she grew scarcely any afterward. "If I could only be five feet tall I would be content," she would complain, standing on her toes and stretching her arms above her head. "But I am afraid I shall never be that tall." And she never was.

But that was not her worst grievance. Every time she looked in her mother's big brass mirror she thought, Oh, why can't I be pretty like Sophia? One day, seeing the lingering typhus spots, she was so disheartened that she didn't even notice her beautiful blue eyes and golden hair. She had a sweet smile, too, and tight-set lips that revealed determination.

Just now those lips were firmly closed in an effort to master her feelings, as she said to herself, "If I can't be pretty, I can at least be useful. I will try to help everybody everywhere just as much as I can, then they'll have to love me."

One day when she was fourteen years old, word passed around that at ten o'clock on April 1, 1764, there would be an eclipse of the sun. Father Herschel had a tub of water placed in the courtyard, and as the ten o'clock hour approached he gathered the family around it. Just what he did with the tub of water she does not explain; possibly he used it as a mirror to avoid looking directly at the sun. He described the movement of the sun and planets and explained why the shadow was creeping over the land. "The moon," he said, "is coming directly between us and the sun, shutting out its light."

"Father was always interested in the stars," Caroline wrote. "He encouraged us all to watch the movements of the heavenly bodies. Often on clear nights he would take us younger children into the street to some spot where the buildings did not hide the sky, and there he would show us the beautiful groups of stars called constellations.

"One night he called us to come out and see a comet. As we gazed at the bright, shining object, with its long tail streaming across the sky, I asked excitedly, 'What is it made of? Where did it come from? And where is it going?'

"Night after night, as we gazed into the star-studded heavens we children would ply him with questions—'Why do some of the stars shine with a bright, steady light and others seem to dance? Why are they of different colors and some of them so much brighter than others? What are the stars, anyway? and how far away are they?' He would tell us about the astronomers who looked into the heavens through an instrument called the telescope that seemed to bring the stars nearer. Doubtless they would be able to answer many of these questions in time."

One day Caroline and William would be *telling* the astronomers what the answers were! But all that was still in the future.

On the next day after the eclipse, Caroline wrote, "The family was thrown into a tumult of joy" by the sudden appearance of William. He had been in England for nearly seven years. It was midday when he arrived. Alexander, who had been appointed town musician, was blowing a *chorale* from the top of the market tower. He soon came home, and the family were all together with only the Griesbachs missing. Father, mother, brothers, and sister gathered around William to hear him tell of his adventures in England.

At first he had earned his bed and a morsel to

eat by copying music for a music shop in London. Looking around for better-paying employment, he had secured the position of leader of the military band at Leeds, and to add to his meager income, he had taught music and conducted public concerts. This kind of work required much traveling. He had bought a horse and traveled on horseback.

Caroline resented being called away to the kitchen while her brother was telling of his travels and hardships. Her mother reminded her that there was work awaiting her which must be performed before another meal could be served. With a heavy sigh she left the group, grumbling to herself, "Why can't I be with my brother, like the rest of them? He will be going away soon and I may never see him again." Nobody saw the salty tears that fell into the dishwater that day.

"O Mother, why do I have to go to school?" she pleaded. "Why can't I stay home while William is here? You know it is confirmation week, and that means that we have to stay an hour after school every day. Can't I stay out just this week?" But such a thing could not be thought of. Then to add to her grief, William took two days to visit Sophia and her family, who by this time were living in a nearby town. Jacob and Alexander went with him, but Caroline had to stay home to help mother with the work.

Early Sunday morning Caroline had to attend the confirmation services at the church, and they lasted all the morning. William tried to give her a little comfort. As she left the house, he said, "Little sister, you look beautiful today." She was wearing a new black silk dress, and in her hand she held a

21

faded bouquet of artificial flowers, the same one that Sophia had carried on her bridal day eleven years before.

Caroline wrote sadly of their parting: "The church was crowded. The Hamburg *postwagen* (mail coach) left at eleven, bearing away my dear brother. It passed within twelve yards of the open door. I could not leave that solemn ceremony even to go to the door and wave good-by. As they passed, the postilion blew a loud blast on his horn." Caroline remembered little of the service that day, for it was smothered under the misery of her heart. "He's gone! He's gone! my best and dearest brother! And I don't know when I shall ever see him again!"

In the afternoon she went for a walk with some of her school companions, but could think of nothing except how lonely she would be at home without her dear William. Jacob and Alexander were fully occupied with their music. But there was little Dietrich, just nine years old, who was interested in bugs and butterflies and all kinds of insects. He loved Caroline with all his heart. And there was mother who worked so hard, and poor, sick father who needed comfort. Caroline set about to bring all the sunshine possible into the home, and soon she forgot her own sorrows.

Chapter 2

Surprise for Caroline

CAROLINE'S MOTHER stood at the kitchen window looking out. Warm sunshine was melting the snow, bringing promise of an early spring; but it could not warm the chill in mother's heart. That day the family had gone together to the garrison church, but when they returned father was not with them. He was quietly lying in the churchyard, his humble lifework ended, his troubles and anxieties forgotten.

"It will be lonely without your father," mother said. "More than that, it will be difficult to pay our bills without his earnings. We cannot get along on what William sends us, and Jacob scarcely earns enough for his own needs." The words were spoken to Caroline, who was busily clearing away the dinner dishes.

There was a dull pain in Caroline's heart too, and bitter thoughts were struggling for expression: Now that father is gone, there is no one left who understands or sympathizes with me, nobody who cares whether I make anything of myself or not. All they care for is the work I can do. So ran her thoughts. But hiding her dismal feelings under a calm exterior, the girl answered with a degree of cheerfulness:

"We'll get along all right, Mother. William is doing better every year, and Alex is coming along. He will be able to take over father's music pupils. Perhaps we can rent a smaller and less expensive apartment, now that father is no longer with us. And, Mother, I should like to learn a profession and earn a little myself."

After his father's death, the oldest son, Jacob, according to custom, had taken his place as head of the household. When his sister's suggestion reached his ears, he announced decidedly: "Caroline had better get all such independent notions out of her head. Her place is in the kitchen, helping her mother," and he might have added, "waiting on me."

Mother seconded his pronouncement: "Caroline, I want you to become a good *hausfrau,* and that is enough for any girl. This higher learning and these extra accomplishments only spoil a girl for the common duties of life." (*Hausfrau* means "housewife.")

Dismally Caroline said to herself: As if I didn't know all that is necessary about housework, from washing windows and scouring pots to waiting on table and acting hostess to Jacob's and Alexander's aristocratic guests! Must I always be a household drudge? The future seemed dark indeed!

Then one day, to her great joy, she found a friend. In an apartment of the house to which they had moved, there lived a young girl who was an invalid. Caroline visited her and found her sitting up in bed making some fancy beadwork.

"Oh, isn't that beautiful!" she exclaimed.

"Do you like it?" the sick girl asked.

"Do I like it?" Caroline said. "I should say I do! It's perfectly lovely! I wish I knew how to make pretty things like that."

"I'll be glad to show you what little I know." The sick girl got out her samples of all kinds of fancywork for Caroline to examine. "Can't you come over for an hour or two every day?" she invited.

"I don't know when I could come, I'm so busy with the housework." Then after a moment's thought, she said with a whimsical smile, "Unless it might be in the morning before the rest of the family are up!"

To Caroline's delight, the sick girl replied, "Come over as early as you like! We can have a little time together every morning."

"But how will I know when you are awake?" Caroline asked.

"Oh, I'll put on a spell of coughing a little louder than usual as a signal for you to come. Neither your family nor mine will think it strange, because they are so accustomed to hearing me cough."

Early the next morning Caroline was awake, waiting for the signal. The two girls became fast friends and spent many an early morning hour over their needlework, exchanging experiences and ideas as they worked, and trying to comfort each other in their troubles. The frail girl knew that her own trials would soon be at an end, for she was dying of tuberculosis. But Caroline dreaded to think of the years stretching ahead for herself.

25

"I never expect to marry," she confided to her friend one day. "My father cautioned me against any thought of such a thing. He said that, as I was neither handsome nor rich, it was not likely anyone would make me an offer, until, perhaps, when far advanced in life, some old man might take me for my good qualities.

"Not that I am eager for marriage," she continued, "if I can make my own living. I should like to take an apprenticeship or learn some profession, that I might not be a burden to my brothers. The only thing that I am now prepared to do is to go out as a housemaid. It isn't that I object to hard work. I am willing to do my share. But to spend *all* my life as a household drudge, scrubbing and scouring and washing and ironing and waiting table!"

"You are right," her friend agreed. "Too much of that kind of work would become tiresome. There ought to be some time for other things."

"I would like a position as governess in a cultured family, but that would require a knowledge of French, and my mother and brother will not permit me to take lessons."

They chatted on, morning after morning, dolefully sometimes, and sometimes cheerfully, glad for each other's company and sympathy. Caroline worked as fast as she could, for she knew that their time together would be short. Not once did she think of the risk she was running of catching tuberculosis, because she knew nothing about germs. Often she would lay out her samples and look them over carefully to be sure that she knew how to make each one just right. "Now I can teach fancywork," she said happily. "It might even help me in getting a position as governess in some family where it would not be important to know French."

Soon after this her girl friend died. Caroline tried again to persuade her mother to let her learn a profession. "Madam Kuster is starting a class in dressmaking and millinery; why can't I attend?" she pleaded. Mother thought the matter over; perhaps it would be a good idea. Finally Jacob gave his consent, with the understanding, however, that Caroline should use these new skills only in making clothes and household linen for the family. She was not to go into any kind of business of her own.

Mother went to see the elegant Madam Kuster. She was too poor to pay the usual fee for instruction. The kindhearted lady consented to receive the girl into her class at a reduced rate of tuition. Caroline tells of her embarrassment:

"I felt greatly humiliated when introduced to twenty-three young ladies all belonging to genteel families. I expected to be kept in the background and treated as an inferior. Imagine my surprise when the entire class, as well as their accomplished instructor, accepted me as one of themselves and made me feel perfectly at home among them! The hours spent every day in class, learning to do useful and pleasant things, brightened all the rest of the day for me. Among the pupils I made several lifelong friends. One was a little girl eleven years old, who was to remember me thirty-five years later when we met in London."

After Caroline learned to do fashionable dressmaking, she was kept so busy sewing for the family that she had little time for music or fancywork.

Encouraging letters came from William in England. He was making friends everywhere. He was organist and music director in the New Octagon Chapel in Bath, a private chapel built for the guests of the fashionable winter resort at the hot springs.

He was becoming well known as a music instructor, and his list of pupils was lengthening. Jacob, who had gone to England to be with him for a few months, was also doing well.

William sent for Alexander and secured him a place in Linley's Orchestra, which played at the resort. Alexander began at once to teach violoncello and to help William with his sacred concerts in the Octagon Chapel. The brothers often talked about their sister Caroline, who they feared was living a dull, humdrum life in Hanover. Alexander told William how well she played the violin and what a good singing voice she had. That set William thinking. "Do you suppose she might be trained as a singer for my choir?" he asked.

"Just the thing! Of course she could!" Alexander fired back. "Her strong soprano voice is just what you need, William! I'm sure that with a few vocal lessons she would do well helping both with your sacred oratorios and your public concerts. Besides," he added, "she's a good cook and housekeeper, and we certainly need one."

William sat right down and wrote home, suggesting that Caroline join them at Bath. "She can take voice lessons and train as a vocalist," he said.

He wrote a special note to Jacob, who had returned to Hanover, asking him to help Caroline improve her singing voice. "And while she is awaiting such time as I can come and fetch her, will you do me the kindness of giving her a few vocal lessons?"

At first the idea pleased everyone who heard about it. Caroline walked with her head in the clouds—until Jacob began to ridicule the whole scheme: "Caroline a singer! at concerts! Whoever heard her sing?" He would not even take the trouble to test her voice. But Caroline was not to be put off easily. She began practicing by herself without any help from Jacob or anyone else. Whenever she could get away alone she would sing, trying to remember everything she had heard her father teach his pupils. "I would imitate the solo parts," she said, *"shake and all,* as I had heard my brothers play them on the violin."

Every day she continued practicing—and hoping. Then one day William was there—in the parlor talking to mother. Could it be that he was really saying the things her ears reported? "Yes, Mother, she can really help me. I know of no one else who can assist me so well. You need not be afraid to let her come with me, Mother! She has a good voice,

and with a little training will do very well. Oh, no!
a short time away from home will not spoil her. I
want to make this a two-year trial. If my plan does
not work out all right by the end of two years, I
promise to bring her safely home."

Although she was twenty-two, Caroline did not
think herself too grown up to comply with her
mother's wishes. Just now she was thinking fast:
I believe mother will consent, but what about Jacob?
How glad I am that he had to go on that errand to
Denmark; he is not here to object to my leaving.

When finally mother consented to let her daughter go, a sudden compunction of conscience almost
overcame the girl's resolution. "How can mother
ever get along without me?" she queried. "Is it right
for me to go and leave her all the housework to do
alone?"

"Don't worry about that. I'll keep mother sup-
plied with extra money so she can hire a maid to
take your place," her generous brother offered.

Thus, at last, everything was arranged. Mother
and Caroline and the youngest brother, Dietrich,
all went with William to visit Sophia and her family. Caroline said her good-bys.

Two weeks after William made his appearance
at the Hanover home, he triumphantly helped Caroline to the high seat on top of the mail coach. Cou-
rageously holding back the tears, she waved farewell to mother and Dietrich as she began the six-day
journey across the flatlands from Hanover to the
Channel coast.

Caroline's heart was full. At last she was with
William, her best and dearest brother. What girl
could be happier?

30

William and Caroline were so happy in each other's company that they scarcely noticed any discomfort sitting bolt upright on the hard, springless seat of the lumbering mail coach. They bumped jauntily along over the rough roads. Nor did they sense the heat of the midsummer sun that poured down on their shelterless heads.

Caroline was captivated with the sights along the way. She had never before been so far from home. They passed cozy farms and green pasturelands dotted with grazing cattle and goats. Occasionally they stopped at post stations to exchange horses.

The two conversed glibly of childhood days, speaking in German, their native tongue. Now and again William would point out some object in passing, pronounce its name in English, and ask Caroline to repeat the word after him.

They came to the land of dikes and windmills and saw boys and girls trudging along the road lugging pails of milk or driving dogcarts loaded with fruits and vegetables or big, yellow cheeses. For the first time in their lives, brother and sister were becoming really acquainted with each other. They had many things to talk about.

Caroline spoke of their father, of his eagerness to leave his family well provided for, and of his disappointment because of the long illness that prevented his doing so.

"But he has left us an inheritance of far greater value than houses and lands," William reminded her. "He has left us an inheritance of a godly life, and he has given all his sons a musical education by which we can earn our own living."

At night they looked up at the skies. Caroline remembered the constellations that her father had pointed out to her in childhood, and William acquainted her with others she had not known. They watched the Big Dipper slowly revolve around the North Star. She recalled how their father used to talk to them about the glory of the heavens. "I wonder whether the many questions that we children asked him will be answered," she queried.

"It may be a long time before we can find the answers to all of them," William said. "But astronomers are learning many things about the universe that were unknown in centuries past. The telescope is bringing the heavenly bodies into clearer view and opening many of their secrets to us."

William could have continued talking about the stars all night, for this was his favorite subject, but Caroline was getting sleepy. She leaned her head against his shoulder and knew nothing more until they stopped at the next post station to exchange horses and drivers. In the morning the stars were out of sight and forgotten. William had many experiences to relate of his early days of struggle in England.

"How hard you must have worked, William, and how carefully you must have saved in order to send us the help you did after father's death!"

"I really was hard up for a while after arriving in England," William said. "In order to add to my small income I conducted private concerts in homes and taught music pupils. I heard that a pipe organ had been built for the parish church at Halifax, so I applied for the position of organist. There were six other applicants. We drew lots to decide the order in which we were to perform. I came on as number three. The second competitor was expert. He flew over the keys with his nimble fingers. Snetzler, the old organ builder, was disgusted. He ran around the church exclaiming, 'He run over te keys like one cat He vil not gif my organ piphes room for to shpeak!'

"When my turn came I played two or three solemn melodies. At the conclusion Snetzler cried out, 'Aye, aye, tish is very goot indeed; I vil luf tish man, for he gifs my piphes room for to shpeak.'

"A friend who was with me wanted to know how I had produced such a full, grand melody. I reached into my waistcoat pocket and brought out two pieces of lead and told him, 'One of these I placed on a lower key of the organ and the other on the octave above. Then by adapting the harmony, I produced the effect of four hands instead of two.'"

Caroline exclaimed, "How I should like to have heard you play! Will I hear you sometime?"

"We have an organ even superior to that one in the Octagon Chapel at the Bath Health Resort. It accompanies the choir in which you will be singing."

"Ach, Wilhelm! how wonderful!"

Although the brother and sister had been happy in each other's company, neither was sorry when the six days' journey came to an end. As they neared the coast, the weather grew cold; a gale arose and whirled Caroline's hat into a canal. They drew up at the landing. An open rowboat was waiting to take them out to the ship lying at anchor.

"Ach, Wilhelm! Do we have to get into that little thing? We shall be drowned!" Caroline clung to William's arm in terror as their light craft bobbed up and down like a cork on the rolling waves.

Even aboard the ship she was not safe. Before reaching the English coast the ship ran into a storm that broke two masts.

In her quaint way Caroline described their arrival at Dover and, later, at London:

At Dover "we were taken in another rowboat and finally dumped on the shore from the backs of two English sailors. After having crawled to one of a row of neat, low houses, we found the party who had arrived before us devouring their breakfast. Several clean-dressed women were cutting slices of bread and butter as fast as they could. One of them went upstairs with me to help me change my clothes. After breakfast we mounted some sort of cart that was to take us to the place where we were to board the stagecoach bound for London. But we had hardly gone a quarter of a mile when the horse ran away with us, overturning the cart with trunk and passengers. My brother, another passenger, and myself were thrown out, I flying into a dry ditch. We picked ourselves up, unhurt except for the fright, and with the assistance of fellow passengers who had come on the packet with us, succeeded in catching the stagecoach for London.

"Eleven days after leaving Hanover, about noon, we arrived at an inn, and took lodging for the night. Here I had a short rest while William tended to some business. As soon as the shops were lighted up in the evening, he took me to see the city. We went first to the optician's, and my brother became so interested in examining their instruments that

34

I do not remember going to any of the other shops. The next day the mistress of the inn lent me a hat of her daughter's and we went to see St. Paul's Cathedral, the Bank, and a few other places of interest. We were never off our legs except for meals at our inn.

"At ten o'clock in the evening we went in the night coach to Bath, where we arrived at four o'clock in the afternoon. Mrs. Bulman, William's landlady, welcomed us. With William acting as interpreter, she told me that she and her husband and daughter occupied the ground floor of the house. There was some conversation between the two, from which I gathered that William was telling her to talk to me as much as possible, since he wanted me to learn to speak the English." (Yet in spite of William's eagerness for his sister to learn English, the two habitually conversed with each other in German.)

"Seeing that I was tired, the landlady showed me to my room on the third floor, and made me understand that the room next to mine was reserved for Alexander when he was home. He was away at the time, filling a musical engagement in Bristol. I went immediately to bed. I was nearly *annihilated* for want of sleep, not having been in a bed for more than two or three nights during the twelve days of our journey. I did not awaken until the next afternoon, when I found my brother had just left his room. We both had slept twenty-four hours."

Chapter 3

The Heavens Come Closer

THE NEXT MORNING when Caroline came down to breakfast, Mrs. Bulman greeted the newcomer with a pleasant smile and started a conversation in English. Caroline nodded and smiled back. Whatever the English lady was saying must be all right. A huge servant stood awaiting orders. Caroline sensed that she was being scrutinized and evaluated, but this did not embarrass her. She could return the compliment. William breezed in.

"Good morning, little sister! I announce the opening of school today. Are you ready to begin your studies?"

"Ja, ja!" Her response was enthusiastic.

Without wasting time, William munched on a slice of toast as he drew a scrap of paper from his pocket and jotted down a few English words for his sister to learn—and a simple problem in algebra. He handed the slip to her. "Here is your first lesson." It was entitled "Little Lessons for Lina, Number One."

After carefully reading it to her, he said, "If you have questions, bring them to me and I will answer them at lunchtime. This is the beginning of your university course. You will study English, higher mathematics, accountancy, and science; and here is a book to keep the family accounts in." He showed her how to make the entries. Caroline was radiantly happy. All she could say was, "Ach, Wilhelm!"

After breakfast they went into the drawing room, which was reserved for private concerts and rehearsals and for William's and Alexander's music pupils. It was a large room, splendidly furnished. The harpsichord stood in one corner. Scattered about the room were William's violin, guitar, oboe, and other musical instruments. Alexander's violoncello occupied an important place.

William handed Caroline a sheet of music. "Try your voice on this, little sister. I'll start you out with two vocal lessons a day." After giving her some exercises to practice, he was away to notify his music pupils that he was back in the country and ready to resume teaching.

Mrs. Bulman appeared and took Caroline into the kitchen. "From that day on," Caroline says, "the first hours immediately after breakfast were spent in the 'kittchen,' where Mrs. Bulman taught me how to make all sorts of 'pudings' and 'pyis,' besides other things that I should never want to make."

Mrs. Bulman understood very little German and never tried to speak it, which was fortunate for Caroline. Within six weeks she could understand and speak English well enough to take over the house-

Mary Bulman and Caroline watched the people in the King's Bath.

hold management. Shopping and marketing were her most difficult tasks. She wrote about her first day at the market:

"I was sent alone among the fisherwomen, butchers, and basket women, and brought home whatever in my fright I could pick up. I did not know at the time that my kind and thoughtful brother, Alexander, who had returned from his summer engagement at Bristol, was following and watching from a distance to make sure that I would reach home safely."

The first few weeks were difficult ones. Everything was so new and different. Caroline struggled against homesickness and depression. The program of practice and study that William outlined for her wore her down.

"You are tired, Caroline. Suppose we drop the algebra for a time," her brother suggested.

"The algebra is not as hard as the arithmetic," she protested. "It's those terrible multiplication tables. I never could learn them!"

"Oh, don't let that worry you; just copy them on a piece of paper and keep them in your pocket for reference." And that is what she did, but she never fully mastered "those terrible multiplication tables."

One day Mrs. Bulman's daughter, Mary, took Caroline to visit the resort. They went first to an outdoor terrace overlooking a warm-water pool, the King's Bath. This was a sort of large swimming pool, open to the sky and surrounded on three sides by the walls of the Pump Room and the other resort buildings. A hundred or more men and women could be seen walking around, immersed up to their

39

necks in the warm water. Each bather had a small floating wooden tray which he pushed before him. On this he laid the articles that he wished to keep by him while in the bath, such as pipe, nosegay, snuffbox, or perfume. Frequently one of the women would take a handkerchief from her tray and wipe the perspiration dripping from her face.

"The bathers do not look as if they are having a very enjoyable time," Caroline observed.

Her companion laughed. "Most of the people you see here bathe for health rather than for pleasure. One of the attractions of the resort is its famous mineral springs. Physicians throughout the country recommend these baths to their patients as a way to recover from their various ills."

After a time the bathers began to leave. At the same time the Pump Room was filling with people.

"What next?" Caroline asked.

"Do you see the man at the bar serving that yellowish water from the large urn? It is mineral water. Each patient is advised to drink three cups every day. The guests come to this room to get it."

Caroline drank one cup, but declined the second.

"Where do the bathers change their suits?" Caroline was a tireless collector of facts, which she usually gathered by questions well asked and answers long remembered.

"As a general thing, the bathers dress in their hotel rooms and then are carried to and from the baths in sedan chairs."

Mary and Caroline next toured the newly built assembly rooms. At the tables handsome youths in velvet and ruffles chatted gaily with daintily dressed maidens sipping tea or ale and listening to the fiddlers. Plumes waved and jewels flashed amid crinolines and flounces and fans. Birthday parties and anniversary parties were in progress, and all manner of games.

Occasionally Caroline caught sight of her brother, moving with graceful dignity among the crowds, bowing to this one and nodding to that, speaking a word of welcome here and a word of business there, smiling at all, but never pausing to listen to their gossip or to notice who were the winners at the gambling tables, or showing interest in the religious discussions or political debates being carried on by various groups scattered about the rooms. His dignified reserve and gracious manner seemed to hold the respect of all.

Occasionally he would take up his violin, and the other fiddlers would join him in a lively and spirited waltz that would start the young couples whirling into the middle of the room, while the older folks would accompany the dancers by beating a tattoo on the floor with their feet.

Mary remarked, "Your brother pays little attention to all these amusements. Why doesn't he stop to enjoy the fun?"

Caroline answered, "I guess it is because his thoughts are so deeply immersed in the realities of living and in his efforts to discover the great mysteries of the universe. Trifling superficialities interest him very little."

While the girls were talking they noticed some of the guests moving toward the door. "As you know, Caroline, this is a festival day, and your brother is giving a sacred concert in the chapel."

"Yes, I know. Shall we go?"

The anthem was greatly enjoyed by the two visitors, especially by Caroline, who knew that William had composed it.

The girls walked home briskly, for it was past the dinner hour.

At the table William asked Caroline, "What do you think of the Bath Health and Pleasure Resort?"

Caroline answered with her usual frankness, "The buildings are elegant, but I would not want to live in that kind of society. I pity people whose chief interest is seeking their own pleasure. I'd much rather be home here with you and Alex, dealing with the realities of living and helping to solve the great problems of the universe. But we greatly enjoyed the anthem you composed, William."

William smiled. "I'm glad of that, for I like to think that my musical contributions add something of value to the resort programs. Perhaps you noticed the portrait of 'Beau' Nash in the Pump Room."

Caroline twisted her face into a smile as she answered, "Yes, indeed, it is so imposing I couldn't miss it."

Then William went on to explain. "Nash did more than any other man to build up the town and improve the resort. He was called the King of Bath. Everyone bowed to his will. But once, more than thirty years ago, he met his match." This is the story as William probably told it to Caroline that evening.

It had been announced that John Wesley, the

great preacher, was coming to speak in the town. Nash threatened all kinds of things if he dared to come, and the ruffians of the town were delighted. Curiosity drew the elite also. Sensing the danger, Wesley's friends tried to persuade him not to appear in public. But Wesley dared not shirk duty. He knew that among the health and pleasure seekers were many invalids who had but little longer to live and who were unprepared for death.

He came to Bath! He stood boldly up before that excited crowd, some of whom were waiting eagerly to see the great preacher humbled. Wesley preached, and it was no soft message that he delivered that day. He warned them all—frivolous pleasure seekers, complacent saints, and debauched sinners alike—of their lost condition, and pleaded with them to accept Christ, their only hope of life eternal. His fearless words, spoken in the power of the Holy Spirit, surprised and awed his hearers.

A solemn hush rested on the audience. Some among them were becoming convicted of their lost condition. They were beginning to think seriously of giving up their sinful lives and seeking the way of salvation. At that moment Nash appeared! Coming up to the speaker, he demanded, "By what authority do you do these things?"

A spirited argument followed between the two. With calm dignity Wesley upheld his right to preach. After a while Nash was unable to find words with which to answer. He turned to the audience and said, "I should like to know what these people came here for."

A woman's voice was heard, speaking from the

crowd. "Mr. Wesley, sir, leave this man to me; let an old woman answer him. You, Mr. Nash, take care of your body; we take care of our souls; and for the food of our souls we come here."

The "King of Bath" quietly walked away and allowed the meeting to proceed.

Wesley's *Journal* shows that he preached in Bath many times afterward and to full audiences.

The winter season of festivities at the resort closed in 1773 with a grand Easter program of concerts and oratorios.

Now, thought Caroline, my dear brother will have some time to be with me. But she was disappointed, for William was so worn out with the winter's work that he would go to bed early, usually with a bowl of bread and milk and a pile of his favorite books.

The books did not look interesting to Caroline. "Why do you have to read all those?" she asked.

"I am studying them in order to learn more about the stars."

"About the stars! What do they have to do with the stars? They look very dry and uninteresting to me, especially that one with angles and triangles and lines and numbers."

"That is trigonometry. Astronomers have to understand trigonometry in order to measure the distances of the planets." He handed her one of the smaller books. "You would find this book by Ferguson interesting. James Ferguson started out as a poor shepherd boy watching sheep. He began his study of the stars lying on his back in the grass at night, and measuring how far apart the stars were with a knotted string. From that beginning he went on to make original experiments by means of simple devices which he invented himself.

"In his book he tells about the motion of the planets around the sun. He describes the Milky Way, that bright, broad path of light that we can see at night extending across the heavens. He tells about a misty spot just below the sword belt of the bright constellation Orion. Ferguson describes it as looking like a 'gap in the sky' through which one may see, as it were, a much brighter region beyond. Lina, I want to get a telescope and see these wonders for myself.

"These long lists of figures are called catalogs." He opened another book. "They list stars and constellations and tell where and when they will appear in the heavens. They look terribly uninteresting, but these catalogs are really very important. I want to do more than locate the constellations and the principal stars in the sky. I want to know what they are, how they are distributed out in space, in what direction they lie from us, and how far they are from one another. I want to know something about the construction of the heavens. For this purpose I must have a telescope."

William rented a small telescope, the best that he could afford, from an optician's shop. But its magnifying power was low. "I shall need an instrument with much higher magnifying power than any I can afford to buy, or even to rent," he said. "Lina, I have about decided that if we are to have a really good telescope, one that will bring the heavenly bodies into close view, we will have to set to work and make one ourselves. So I have sent to London for lenses, and now I want you to use some strong pasteboard to make a tube into which we can fit these lenses. In this way we shall rig up a good telescope of our own. Someday I shall be making my own lenses. That is the reason why I am studying this little book on optics. It deals with light and color, with lenses, opera glasses, and telescopes. If I am to make telescopes I must know how to shape the lenses and how to arrange them inside the tube of the telescope so as to obtain the highest possible magnifying power."

Caroline was becoming alarmed. William was losing his interest in music. Astronomy was all he could talk about. She was not the least bit interested in astronomy. The stars were doing all right—they could take care of themselves. She wanted to finish her musical education. She wanted to become a prima donna and take part in concerts and oratorios. She wanted to make her mark in the world. But William wanted to look at stars!

Caroline took some of her precious practice time and went to work to help her brother make a telescope. But when they tried to see Jupiter through their homemade instrument they could scarcely get a glimpse of the bright planet. The four-foot pasteboard tube was not stiff enough to stay in a straight line.

Nothing daunted, William said, "I think tin tubes will work better; I'll have some made. Perhaps Alexander can help us with them in his spare time." William examined his small rented telescope to see how it was put together. He bought tools, books of instructions, and a quadrant, which is an instrument for measuring a star's angle above the horizon. "I'll do some experimenting," he said.

By the beginning of summer nearly all William's music pupils had left Bath. Now, at last, we can have some time together, thought Caroline. But again she was disappointed. One day when she went into the drawing room for her music practice she found a cabinetmaker constructing a tube and making telescope stands of all descriptions.

Tools, materials, and telescope parts were strewn about over the elegantly furnished drawing room. The harpsichord groaned under a weight of globes, maps, lenses, and reflectors.

Caroline looked around in dismay. "What has become of that pile of music I was copying?"

Alexander pointed to a corner of the room. "Over there on top of William's guitar."

"What about the rehearsal we were to have this afternoon?"

"Oh, go ahead, it won't bother us."

"Alex, how can we carry on our musical practice in all this confusion?"

But there was no other way! The whole house was turned topsy-turvy. Amid the continual grind of work, Caroline would snatch a few hours for her lessons and vocal practice, and William would squeeze in a little time for composing anthems and chants and hymn tunes for his chapel choir, or solos for his concert singers. These would be needed in a few months when the winter season opened again at the resort.

"What are you intending to do with all that junk?" Caroline had found William in the act of unloading a boxful of all sorts of things—hones, polishers, gadgets, tools of every description—right there in her immaculate sitting room. Someone had told him about a man who was engaged in the business of making and polishing mirrors, but who had grown tired of the job and was selling out. William had immediately hunted up the man and had purchased his entire stock of tools and patterns and half-finished mirrors. Caroline looked on in dismay as he spread out the conglomerate mass on table and chairs and finally on the floor. He drew out of the pile an old, torn notebook.

"Patterns and formulas, I do believe! And here is one for making white metal! Just what I need!" William had decided to use the reflecting type of telescope. For these he must have more perfect reflectors than any he had yet been able to obtain. He needed the very best formulas for the metal mixtures that were to produce the mirrors.

"Don't you see, Lina, everything is contributing to my success, even this pile of junk!" She subsided. Her brother was irrepressible.

In the autumn William had to take up his duties again as organist and choir leader. He also had ten or more private music pupils.

Alexander was as handy at tools and as clever at inventing as William. Whenever he was home between his musical engagements, which kept him at Bristol much of the summer, he would help William construct mountings for his homemade telescopes, with brackets for holding the lenses, and slides for adjusting the focus inside the tubes. He also made different kinds of contrivances for moving the tube up and down or from side to side, so as to point it toward the particular spot in the heavens that he wished to view.

In his bedroom Alexander set up a huge turning

machine which he had brought from Bristol for the purpose of shaping eyepieces and making parts for grinding lenses.

William worked on patiently. He would put a telescope together in one way, then make the next one a little different. At night he would try them out to see which was the best, and he kept a careful record of each one and of how well it worked. He tried various styles of tubes and different arrangements of lenses and mirrors inside.

After more than a hundred experiments he achieved success. He produced a Newtonian reflector that gave him a better view of the stars than any of the telescopes he had found in the shops. It had a magnifying power of 222. He pointed it toward Orion, adjusted the focus, and took a long and satisfying look. He called his sister.

A scene of dazzling beauty met her eye. Multitudes of stars they had not seen before now came into sight, and there shone the misty, milky nebula, with its variations of brightness, and a group of stars within it.

"Ach! Wilhelm! How wonderful! How beautiful!" she cried.

"Yes, indeed! Glorious and marvelous are the works of the Eternal!" William's own telescope, which he had made himself, brought Saturn so near that they could plainly see the planet and its rings. That night William's ambition for telescope making received a tremendous impetus; and never after that did Caroline wonder why her brother was fascinated by the study of the heavens.

But the expanding telescope industry demanded more space. So one day the Herschels and the Bulmans packed the contents of the music studio and workshops and moved to a larger house. It was near the Walcot Turnpike and was known as the Walcot House. It had several workshops attached, and there was garden space at the back suitable for setting up the telescopes, also a flat roof which was convenient for observing. Yet even here there was scarcely room for all the paraphernalia that the brothers hunted up to help them in their telescope making.

Caroline's time was as fully occupied as was William's, with cooking and entertaining and daily vocal practice and music copying. She was getting ready to take a leading part in the oratorios. Her brother thought it important that she should become acquainted with social etiquette. But Caroline saw no need for this kind of education. He argued with his stubborn little sister: "If you are to appear on the stage before a cultured audience, you should cultivate a graceful and pleasing manner."

She protested. "The artificial, affected manners of these gay idlers who attend the resort seem utterly contemptible to me. I do not wish to copy them." Her brother finally won out and hired a lady teacher to give her lessons—"to drill me for a gentlewoman," as she expressed it.

Chapter 4

A Brand-new Planet

ONE EVENING William came home from the resort with a tremendous piece of news: "Linley has resigned his position as conductor of the Bath concerts, and the position has been offered me."

Caroline could not conceal her delight. "That means that you will have to lighten up on your star study and give all your attention to music, doesn't it?"

"Perhaps that may be necessary for a time," William said. "The most serious thing about it is that we shall be losing the best soprano we have, Linley's daughter Elizabeth. It means, too, that I shall have to call upon my little sister to take Elizabeth's place as first soprano."

"What! Do you mean that I shall have to follow the beautiful and talented Elizabeth Linley! They say she has sung in public ever since she was a child."

Caroline was overwhelmed. It had

all come about so suddenly! She had been singing in the choir for some time, but to be asked to fill the position of leading soloist——

"But, my dear, isn't that what you have always wanted to be—a prima donna? I thought you would be pleased."

"Yes, of course, it is what I still want to be, but not so soon! Not just yet! How can I?"

"Oh, you will do all right. You will have several months to get ready."

"I will do my best," she said, and she doubled her practice hours.

The oratorio season just before Easter arrived. Caroline took the soprano solos in *Messiah, Judas Maccabeus,* and *Samson,* while William conducted the choir. She had been working for weeks, copying the orchestral parts for ninety players, besides the scores for all the soprano singers. As she gathered the copied pages, she kept turning the question over in her mind, "Does William approve of my efforts? Is there anything more I could do to make his work a greater success?" After the final rehearsal the question was still in her mind. As William stepped to her side to escort her to the carriage waiting outside he whispered, "You did well with those difficult solos; have no fears; you are doing all right!"

Tired? Why had she even thought she was tired! Those encouraging words from the brother she loved drove all her weariness away. She was ready to tackle anything, any kind of job that William needed done.

The work program at the Herschel home continued growing more and more strenuous. Often William would dash out of the assembly room at the resort, race home to his workshops, then rush back with all speed in time to perform his next part on the program. According to his sister, "Every leisure moment was eagerly snatched for resuming some work which was in progress, and many a lace ruffle was torn or bespattered with molten pitch in his haste. My time was much taken up with attending on my brother when polishing, since by way of keeping him alive I was obliged to feed him by putting the food into his mouth bit by bit. Once, in order to finish a seven-foot mirror, he did not take his hands from it for sixteen hours together, as no interruption in this particular task of polishing could be permitted. I would often sit by his side and read aloud from his favorite authors while he made his skillful strokes. He was never unemployed at meals, but while eating was always contriving or making drawings."

(Nowadays telescopes are measured according to the *diameter* of the large mirror. William Herschel measured his telescopes by the *focal length* of the mirror—the distance from a mirror or lens to the point where the image is in sharp focus—which was almost the same as the length of the tube.)

One clear night William carried his seven-foot telescope into the street in front of the house. He was deeply engrossed in making observations when he heard footsteps approaching and a voice spoke to him from out of the shadows: "What are you doing out here on this cold night?"

"I am trying to estimate the height of the mountains on the moon."

"How are you doing that?"

"By measuring the shadows they cast."

53

When William took his eye from the telescope the stranger asked, "May I have a look?"

"Certainly, with pleasure."

The man speaking was William Watson, Jr. He stepped to the eyepiece.

"This is thrilling. I have never before seen so clear a view of the moon. What a splendid instrument you have here! I am told that you make your own telescopes. I must tell my friends about this."

Watson called on the Herschels the next day. "We are organizing a literary and philosophical society here in Bath. We shall meet to read papers on scientific subjects, and we invite you to join us."

Watson came again and again to visit the Herschels and brought with him many interested friends to look through the telescopes.

Herschel joined the Literary and Philosophical Society of Bath and began at once sending in papers on a variety of scientific subjects. These papers were essays in which he reported his scientific experiments and his observations through the telescope, with his findings and conclusions. They were called *Philosophical Transactions*. After his study of the moon he wrote an essay on his lunar observations and gave it to his friend Watson, who put it into the hands of Sir Joseph Banks, who at that time was president of the Royal Society of London.

One day Sir Joseph called to exchange ideas with William. He brought with him Dr. Nevil Maskelyne, head of the Greenwich Observatory. Caroline listened intently to the astronomical discussions that resounded through the house that day. She was elated to hear her amateur brother taking part in a spirited controversy with two renowned scientists, and holding his own part of the discussion very well. Yet neither personal association with men of distinction nor the honors shown William could spoil or change in the least the sensible, unpretentious, hard-working German sister.

She laughed whimsically when William said, "I can't understand how it is that you feel so perfectly at home among these important people, when you act so shy and awkward among the folks that you meet at the resort."

"I sometimes wonder myself," she said. "The truth is that trying to make conversation about nothings is drudgery for me. Many of the women at the resort seem so empty-headed; the girls laugh and simper and giggle. To me they seem little better than idiots. The men talk about games and races and petty politics. But I enjoy the company of these scientists, who are studying and working to learn all they can about the universe around us. Every time I talk with them or hear them talk with you, I learn something new and interesting."

Soon after this, William began a "systematic review of the heavens." He would map out a path and follow it across the sky, pointing his telescope toward each of the principal stars that passed the field of vision in his telescope, and trying to learn all that could be known about each particular star. He measured the comparative brightness of thousands of stars, and noted those that differed in color. Some seemed to glow with a pure white light, others shone with a red glow, or orange, yellow, or blue. He made a careful record of all that he saw through his telescope. He was making his own catalog of the sky!

These telescope journeys were called *sweeps*. A complete journey over the entire visible sky consisted of many sweeps, and was called a *review of the heavens*. Caroline was now spending more and more time with William at the telescopes, and was becoming fascinated with what they revealed.

One day in 1781, after several moves, William said, "Lina, I think we shall have to move back to our old place, 19 New King Street. I miss the convenient places we had there for setting up the telescopes near the house."

"What! Move again so soon! We've scarcely gotten over our last move, hardly more than a year ago, and now to go through all the trouble of packing and moving and settling! Oh, William!" Caroline didn't grumble often, but this seemed a little more than she could take.

"I know it's hard on you, Lina, but I cannot spare the time to go over to the garden whenever I need to use the larger instrument. I must have my telescopes close together so that I can move quickly from one to another and get the very best view possible during the precious moments when the sky is clear and the atmosphere right for observing."

It was true. William needed more room for his telescopes. So back to New King Street they moved, furniture, instruments, tools, and all. Without the loss of one night, William set up his seven-foot telescope and continued his review of the heavens. He had now completed his first review and was starting his second. Caroline remained behind to finish some business.

When she arrived at New King Street, William had news for her. "I think I have discovered a new comet! It must be a very distant one; it is so pale that I could only faintly see it."

"What made you think it was a comet? How did you know it was not a very distant star?"

"Because it had shape, presented a round surface. It is not just a point, like the stars. I tried several different eyepieces and every time I used one of higher power the image grew larger, and I could see plainly that it has a disk. The stars, as you know, never show form or shape, but always appear to us merely as points of light." (In his various instruments William used magnifying powers varying from 227 to 2,010.)

William watched this strange object again several nights later and noticed that it seemed to change its position slightly among the other stars in the sky. That was another indication that it was not a distant star. It must be some object near enough to the earth so that its change of position could be observed. He decided it must be a comet. If not a comet, what else could it be?

Of course, he told his friend Watson about this "new comet." Watson immediately sent word to the observatories in Greenwich and Oxford. The astronomers there began searching for it with their telescopes. William wrote them, giving its exact location in the sky. He wrote a paper entitled "Account of a Comet." It was read to the Royal Society at London.

"A queer comet," some observed, "without any tail or any haziness! It cannot be a comet! It must be something else!"

"Very different from any comet I ever saw or heard of," Dr. Maskelyne wrote to Watson. Later he said in a letter to Herschel, "It is likely to be a regular planet in an orbit around the sun." And that is what it proved to be, another planet in our family of worlds, circling our sun, a giant sister to our little world, and so far away that eighty-four of our years are required for it to complete one journey around the sun. William Herschel, Caroline's favorite brother, was the first man to discover the seventh planet.

"How strange that none of the leading astronomers discovered it before!" Caroline commented.

Her brother corrected her: "Not at all strange, Lina; it is so far away and appears so small that, though doubtless seen many times, it has not been noticed in particular. I should not have found it myself had I not taken time to examine every object that moves across the field of vision in my telescope and to keep a record of the position of each one in the sky."

It was not long before astronomers everywhere were talking about Herschel's "new star." They continued to watch its nightly journeys across the sky, along with the other stars, and they noticed that it changed its position very slightly from night to night. After a time it dropped low out of sight and could not be seen at any time of the night. Late the following summer it appeared again, and scores of telescopes were turned toward it. Astronomers were trying to calculate its course by watching the changes in its position. They finally all agreed that it must be a planet, another member of our solar system.

Herschel's name was now in all the leading journals of Europe. Before the end of the year he was called to London and awarded the annual prize medal. But he was not thinking of the fame that his discovery had won him; he was filled with a sense of reverence for the One who had created these myriad suns and worlds. He said, "I had gradually perused the great volume of the Author of nature, and was now come to the page which contained a seventh planet."

William wanted the new planet to be named Georgium Sidus after King George; but Bode, one of the leading astronomers, said it should be called Uranus.

The Herschel home was becoming less and less a music conservatory and more and more a telescope-manufacturing plant. That summer, after the first discovery of the new planet, William began talking about constructing a thirty-foot telescope.

He needed a larger instrument, one that would admit more light, equipped with more powerful lenses and a larger reflecting mirror than any that he then had. But where could he find a mechanic who would cast the thirty-six-inch disk required for the large mirror? None of the foundries in Bath or Bristol would undertake to make one so large. He decided that he would have to make it himself. So he had a furnace built in the basement of the house.

The mold for the disk was to be made of horse dung, a material that is very hard when dry and does not soften under heat. Bushels of this material had to be pounded in a mortar and then sifted through a fine sieve. Caroline undertook this task. It was the work of several days. She pounded and pounded until her arms ached. Sir William Watson dropped in to see what was going on.

The melted metal ran out of the ash hole, the flagstones began to ex-
plode, and *** men ran for their lives.

"You must be tired; let me assist you," he volunteered.

"Yes, a little tired. Alex helps when he is around, but he is not here just now." Her visitor took the pestle from her hand and pounded awhile.

In a few days the mold was finished and the molten metal poured. (Nowadays glass is often used to make large telescope mirrors, but in the 1780's no one thought of using that. The Herschels were using mixtures of different kinds of metals.) Something was wrong! The liquid metal was dripping through a crack in the bottom of the mold. When cooled, the cast was thinner on one side than on the other and too badly cracked to be of any use. William diagnosed the trouble: "That last formula is at fault," he said. "In our effort to make the mirror strong enough to resist bending, we used too large a percentage of tin in the mixture. We will have to try again."

"Yes, we'll have to try again!" sighed Caroline. She began once more the tedious work of preparing material for another mold. The formula for the metal was changed; more copper was used and less tin.

"It ought to be all right this time." William was confident. But again he was disappointed. Later he wrote what happened at this second trial:

"When everything was ready we put our 537 pounds of metal into the melting oven and gradually heated it. Before it was sufficiently fluid for casting, we noticed that some small quantity began to drop through the bottom of the furnace into the fire. The crack soon increased, and the metal came out so fast that it ran out of the ash hole, which was on a level

61

with the stone floor. When it reached the pavement the flagstones began to crack and some of them began to blow up, so that we found it necessary to keep a proper distance and allow the metal to make its own course." The way they kept their "proper distance," as Caroline tells it, was to run for their lives:

"Both my brothers and the caster and his men were obliged to run out at opposite doors, for the stone flooring flew about in all directions as high as the ceiling. My poor brother fell exhausted by heat and exertion on a pile of brickbats."

Further efforts to make a thirty-foot telescope were abandoned for a time. However William and Alexander kept on experimenting at telescope making. At night William and Caroline also spent much time observing. On cloudless nights they would sometimes remain at the telescopes until the stars faded into the dawn. Then, after a few winks, William would be off to teach his music pupils.

Inside the house, Caroline would start the domestic machinery going, then lie down for a few hours' sleep. After that she might go into the shop where Alexander was making various gadgets and hand-worked machinery for adjusting the telescopes. If her help was not needed there, she would sit down to file William's letters, or perhaps begin revising a star catalog, adding William's more recent discoveries to the lists already made by other astronomers. Or it might be to copy the latest paper he was preparing to send to the Royal Society.

Copying these papers was no small task. Caroline wrote a smooth, even hand, and so careful was she that in all the hundreds of documents she copied or computed during her lifetime, only two or three minor mistakes were ever found, and these were in her last work, done when she was growing old.

Once she asked William, "What is the use of writing all these papers?" and William gave a carefully thought-out answer:

"I want my fellow astronomers to have the benefit of the knowledge I have gained; it may help them in making further investigations. We are all interested in assisting one another, hoping someday to solve the mystery of the stars."

Worldwide interest brought many visitors to the Herschel home requesting the privilege of viewing the newly discovered planet through a telescope made by the one who had discovered the planet. Nobles, dukes, princes, noted scientists, and university teachers—Caroline enjoyed entertaining them all with astronomical information. She would explain the movements of the planets and the mechanism of the instruments with equal skill. The guests would compare the qualities of Herschel's latest telescopes, and before leaving would often place an order for an instrument.

Caroline kept all William's records in good order. She knew that as soon as he completed this second review of the heavens he would immediately start another.

Copying and arranging these records was a tedious task, but Caroline put her whole heart into it. She was happy, for she was helping William, just as he was helping his fellow astronomers in solving the mystery of the stars.

Chapter 5

At the King's Court

LINA, CAN YOU gather the mu sical parts for this evening's performance? The chaise is at the door, waiting to take us to Bristol for the rehearsal."

It was William speaking. Another resort season was closing for the summer.

In the midst of the excitement, who should appear but George Griesbach, one of Sophia's sons who was musician to Her Majesty Queen Charlotte, wife of King George III. He brought word that William was expected in London, and should bring one of his telescopes with him.

As soon as William could get away from his work at the resort, he packed his seven-foot telescope, his star atlas and catalogs, his micrometer, and whatever else was required, and took the stagecoach for London. For the seven-foot telescope he had made a special kind of stand that could be taken apart and put together quickly.

"Don't get lonesome, Lina, and don't work too hard; I'll be back in a few days." A wave of the hand, and William was gone.

In London he was met by his friend Watson, and entertained at the home of Watson's father, Sir William Watson, who was physician to King George. Back in Bath, Caroline waited expectantly, wondering what this trip might mean for William.

The "few days" went by, then a few more days, but no William came home. Instead came a letter saying, "Please send my black suit and some money."

Watson brought word that the king often talked with William at the court.

William at the court! William at the king's court! What did it all mean?

Caroline waited. Again William sent for money, and again she sent it.

Then came another letter. William was spending days at the Greenwich Observatory with Dr. Maskelyne, Mr. Aubert, and other astronomers. One sentence in the letter particularly pleased her: "They seem to be delighted with my seven-foot, and some have openly stated that it is the best telescope they have seen thus far."

He wrote again, telling of evenings spent with the royal family at Windsor, also of dining with Lord Palmerston, Sir Joseph Banks, and with governors, officials, and distinguished scientists.

Later he wrote of entertaining the princesses and some of their lady friends in the queen's apartment. He had made an artificial planet, because the weather was too cold and wet for the ladies to go outside.

Caroline continued to wait for her brother's homecoming and to wonder what the outcome of his visit to London might be. Two full months passed before her curiosity was satisfied. Then William suddenly appeared with the startling announcement: "King George wants me to give up my musical profession and devote all my time to astronomy. He has appointed me to be his private astronomer, and has set aside an annual allowance of 200 pounds for my support. This means, of course, that it will not be long before we shall be moving to London."

Caroline was dumfounded. "Move to London! Go away from Bath! Give up your musical career now, when your future here looks so promising! Why, William, you are reaching the height of your success. And now to leave it all—our friends, our musical prospects! Move to a new place! Take up a new profession!"

William's answer showed how little all this meant to him. "But just think what it will mean, Lina. I can spend all my time exploring the heavens! No more distractions! No more interruptions with music lessons and rehearsals! My duties will be light. The king has asked me to give the princesses lessons in astronomy, and has told me to be ready whenever I am called upon to stage demonstrations for the royal family and their guests. We shall be expected to receive at our home any of their friends who may wish to look through the telescopes. Can you think of any occupation more desirable, more delightful?"

"But 200 pounds a year, William—how can we live on that? The 400 you are earning now isn't any more than we need."

"Don't worry about the small income, little sister. I asked permission of the king to make and sell telescopes, and he graciously gave his consent. Telescope making ought to be a profitable business because so many people are interested in star study these days. Best of all, I shall be gaining an experience. By making telescopes for others, I shall be perfecting my skill, and in the end I shall have more perfect instruments for my own use. Someday I may succeed in making one so powerful that I can actually discover the arrangement of this great universe in which we live. Perhaps someday I shall be able to prove that the stars are distant suns, as I already believe. Perhaps I shall learn how they are distributed in space. It may be that someday I shall realize my hope and *discover the construction of the heavens.*"

To Caroline, this sudden change in her brother's plans meant either a separation from him or an end to all her most cherished ambitions. Already she had received flattering offers from concert conductors. But she could not be persuaded to lend her talents to anyone but William. Could she now give up all her fond dreams and turn from the goal toward which she had been striving for ten years, ever since she had left her home in Hanover? Could she do all this for the brother she loved? An immediate decision must be made. She left the room. When she returned her answer was ready. She would do it! She would go with her brother to London, or to any other place in the world. She would stay with him as long as he needed her; and he must not know how much it hurt.

"You are in a grand enterprise, William, and I will stand by you as long as I can help you," she beamed, no hint of disappointment or regret in her voice or on her face.

William smiled. Without wasting words on sentiment, he asked, "Can you get things ready for packing right away? Alex will be here soon to help."

Their friend Watson came to assist them. He had spent many pleasant hours in the Herschel home. They would miss him, as he would miss them. It was Watson who had told Dr. Maskelyne and Sir Joseph Banks about William's discoveries, and they had told the king.

A few days after this, hired carts stood in the yard at 19 New King Street, Bath, loaded with telescopes, tools, materials, and the family's household goods, ready to leave for London at two o'clock in the morning. William went by stage, and Caroline and Alexander followed the next day. They lodged that night at an inn in Datchet, a village not far from Windsor where they intended to make their home. In the morning they all walked over to inspect the house that William was planning to move into. It was an old deserted hunting lodge. At the back was a large neglected garden and several dilapidated outbuildings.

William was exuberant. "Here we are! This is to be our future observatory! There is plenty of room in these stables for constructing and grinding! We can set up the telescopes on this large grass plot, and we can refit this laundry room for a library in which to keep our books and records. It will be handy, opening as it does into the garden."

They watched the unloading of the carts. Alexander agreed that William had found exactly the right place. But Caroline was dubious. She walked toward the house, where an old woman, the gardener's wife, was waiting to show her around. Her thoughts were none too cheerful as they passed from one room to another.

"So this is to be our home, this ramshackle old place!" she grumbled. "Look at those streaks on the wall where water has run down! Evidently the roof leaks. That accounts for the smell of rotting wood." The old woman admitted that the house did leak a little, but only when it rained, and that wasn't every day.

When the brothers came in for something to eat, they had to listen to Caroline's complaints. William quickly brushed them aside. "Oh, don't mind that, little sister, we can put up with the old house as long as the yard offers such excellent places for observing and there are so many sheds suitable for workshops."

"No time for grumbling!" said Alexander. "You ought to be thankful I am alive! A few minutes ago, while I was pacing the garden, looking for good places to set up the telescopes, I nearly fell into an open well that was overgrown with weeds."

"How horrible! If we stay here we shall soon all be dead," cried Caroline.

William laughed. "No danger of that! I called the gardener and he has cut down the weeds, and I shall see that carpenters put the house in good repair."

He left Caroline to unpack and settle, with the

help of the gardener's wife, while he hurried back to Bath. He was planning to construct a new twenty-foot telescope, and he needed a large mirror for it. The cast for this mirror must be made before the furnace should be taken out of the house they had left. Alexander remained at Datchet to make foundations for setting the telescopes on.

For two months Caroline performed her household duties amid the confusion of building, surrounded by brick, mortar, and timbers, and with the clatter of hammers and the shouts of men ringing in her ears. To add to her troubles, the servant that had been engaged did not appear. She had been jailed on a charge of theft, and it was several weeks before another could be found.

At last the carpentering was finished, the roof mended, windows repaired, doors rehung, and the whole house was smiling under a fresh coat of varnish and paint. The abrupt stillness following the departure of the workmen was even more shattering to Caroline's nerves than the hubbub had been. She was lonesome. The big, empty house seemed a dreary place. Her two brothers seldom came in from the workshops except at mealtime. William discerned beneath her forced and studied smiles an inner misery. It did not take him long to find out what caused it. Caroline had given up her musical career with its crowded program, and for the first time in her life she had unoccupied moments in which to be lonesome.

"Lina, how would you like to make some discoveries on your own?" he asked one day. "Among my finished telescopes there is a small reflector fitted out as a *finder.* We will set it up in the garden and you can search for comets."

Caroline accepted the suggestion and went to work at once, although she considered standing alone at a telescope watching stars somewhat boring. Frequently William would take his seven-foot telescope to the queen's lodge to show celestial objects of special interest to the royal family. At such times Caroline was left alone on the grass plot without another person to talk to. At first the darkness, the silence, and the evening chill increased her feeling of aloneness. However, after a while the first intensive interest in stargazing died away at the queen's lodge, and William was called less frequently and had more time at home. With her brother nearby, Caroline began to take greater pleasure in watching the stars—"minding the heavens," as she called it. After she had made a few discoveries herself, she became so fascinated with the sky that it was nearly as difficult to drag her away from her telescope as it was to dislodge her brother from his.

In October the Bath resort season opened again, and Alexander had to return to his musical duties. Before the end of the following spring he had found a wife and had established a home. After that he spent less time with his brother and sister at Datchet. It was only occasionally now that William could be persuaded to spare a few moments from his work to take his violin from its case and ply the bow while Caroline sang the old, sweet concert solos upon which she had bestowed so many hours of practice.

During the winter months the Thames valley where the house was situated was cold and damp. There were times when the river waters would overflow and cover the ground at the lower end of the garden. On some nights moisture would condense on the tubes of the telescopes and run down in trickles. William was plagued with fever. Yet in spite of his sickness, he made and sold many telescopes that winter.

Alexander joined them during the summers. He made the brass eyepieces and the screws and gadgets for holding and moving lenses and mirrors inside the tube, but William usually insisted on doing the shaping and polishing of the mirrors himself. He had experimented with various strokes until he had learned how to bring each mirror to a state of perfection where it would reflect a perfect image. Occasionally he allowed Caroline to help him.

Handsome prices were paid for the Herschel telescopes. "Who do you think is my best customer?" William asked his sister one day. "It is none other than His Majesty the King. He has ordered five ten-foot telescopes and is paying me £787 10s for them. This one order for telescopes will bring us in an amount of money that nearly equals my royal allowance for four years. Are you still worrying about our income?"

Caroline had to admit that her household budget was ample, but she never did fall in love with the ramshackle old house, and she was always worrying about her brother's health.

Life at Datchet was no less strenuous than it had been at Bath. Observing the sky and manufacturing telescopes more than filled the hours previously devoted to music.

There was one thing that greatly pleased Caroline. Whenever her brother needed help—someone to check the clocks or to assist with the measurements, measure the ground between the observer and the micrometer or to write down memoranda or fetch and carry instruments or perform any other service—he would call on her in preference to anyone else. She said, "I had the comfort to see that my brother was satisfied with my endeavors to assist him."

One day he said to her, "Lina, if you could record my observations from dictation, you could be a still greater help to me. When I take my eye from the telescope to write down what I have seen, I never know how much of importance I may be missing during those few minutes. Then, too, when I return to the eyepiece, I may lose other valuable scenes while my eyes are adjusting to the light. Now, if you could record my observations from dictation, I could continue watching the sky while you are recording what I report to you. Then I would be in less danger of losing scenes of importance."

"I'd love to do that for you," she said. "But could I? I don't think I know enough about stars yet."

"Then," said William, "let's have our first lesson now. Astronomers identify stars by their position in the sky. We use a celestial map, which is the map of the heavens."

Seeing that she was listening closely, he went on. "You understand how to locate cities on a map of the earth by degrees of longitude and latitude.

73

If we know the longitude and latitude of a certain city, we can easily and quickly find it on the map. The position of stars on the celestial map is indicated by what are called degrees, minutes, and seconds of declination (instead of latitude); and by degrees, minutes, and seconds of right ascension (instead of east longitude)."

That was the first lesson. There were more difficult things for Caroline to master. She sighed as she saw William get out his old dust-covered books, those horrid, dry, uninteresting old books filled with problems in algebra and geometry and trigonometry. Resolutely she went to work. Whenever her brother came in sight, she had a question ready for him to answer or a problem for him to help her solve. Often she wondered if in the end she would ever be able to save him more time than she was now costing him. She entered all his answers and solutions in her *Commonplace Book.* In spite of her best efforts she was never able to memorize the tables and formulas for calculating and recording the positions of the heavenly bodies, for changing sidereal (star) time into mean sun time, or for making tables of motion. She copied all the necessary information and kept it handy for reference, along with the multiplication tables. After diligent and persevering study, she became quite expert in recording William's dictations and in calculating the motions of the heavenly bodies.

"Now," said William, "you are due to receive the title 'astronomer's assistant.'"

One day he followed her into the library. "Lina," he said, "I have nearly completed my third review of the heavens. Thus far it has resulted in some remarkable discoveries."

Caroline felt pride swelling inside her. This famous astronomer was *her* brother!

In little more than a whisper, as if scarcely daring to speak of it, William said, "Lina, my next paper will astonish the world. In it I shall announce the most remarkable discovery that I have ever made—*our sun with all its attendant planets is steadily traveling through space!* I have waited until I could be certain of this fact before making any public statement regarding it. Some of my fellow astronomers have hinted at the possibility of such a thing, but so far as I know I am the first to prove it."

Caroline shook her head. "How can you be so sure about it? Didn't the astronomer Tobias Mayer say that if the earth were traveling through space, the stars toward which we are moving would appear to be getting farther and farther apart, and those we are leaving behind would appear to be getting nearer and nearer together?"

"That is what he said, and it is true. If you and I were passing through a forest, the view in front of us would open up, the trees would seem to be getting farther apart as we approached them, and the road would appear to widen. As we moved forward, the view behind would close in. The trees would appear to be getting closer together and the road would seem to grow narrower, till finally it would drop back into the vanishing point. We would know that the trees we were passing did not move. We were the ones that were moving. Now I have proved beyond a doubt that this earth on which we live is steadily moving through space. I have been watching the stars in the constellation of Hercules and have observed that they are widening out; they appear to be getting farther and farther apart. This is because the earth is moving toward them. At the same time the stars in an opposite group are closing in. They seem to be getting nearer and nearer together, because the earth is moving away from them. This convinces me that the sun and the planets that circle it are traveling steadily in that direction."

Caroline almost exploded. "William, if anybody except you had suggested such a thing, I would have said he was crazy. That is what people will think about you when you tell them."

"Yes, I know! A few hundred years ago the authorities might have thrown me into a dungeon or taken off my head for daring to suggest it. But now that we have powerful telescopes, our astronomers can see for themselves indisputable proof that the sun with this earth and all the other planets belonging to our sun's family is steadily traveling through space."

Caroline was still incredulous. "If this is true," she asked, "why has it not been discovered before?"

"Because these stars—these bright shining suns—are so far from us that their change of position among the other stars in the sky is so slight as to be scarcely detected."

Doubtless William explained to his sister that some stars that seem to be very close together are really very far apart, with vast empty spaces between them. If their position is marked on a celestial map the way cities are placed on a map of the world, there may not be the thickness of a hair between them, when really they are separated by millions of miles away out there in space. That is why their change in position on the celestial map is so slight as to be scarcely noticed.

It was only by comparing recent records with those made in former years that any change in the position of the stars could be noted. By comparing a star's present position among the other stars in the sky with the records others had made of its position in past years, he could detect its slightest change of position. But that slight change of position in the sky showed that the star had traveled millions of miles through space.

This whole thing was such a big new idea that Caroline was startled. So were the astronomers who heard William's essay when it was read before the Royal Society. They began to wonder: Are all the thousands of stars that we call *fixed stars*—are they all suns like our sun with planets revolving around them, as the planets in our solar system revolve around our sun?

Herschel had offered evidence to prove that there are really no fixed stars, no stars that do not move; all are traveling through space at tremendous speeds. All are held in space by the same power that keeps the earth, with Mars, and Venus, and Jupiter, and all our sister planets swinging around the sun—the power of gravity.

This discovery had been made possible by William's minute and accurate observations during his long nights at the telescope. When Caroline heard him say that he could not have done this without the help of his untiring little secretary, who had kept the records so carefully, her heart was warmed. She was glad that she had relinquished her ambitions to be a famous singer in order to help her brother accomplish such an important work.

The following summer Alexander was again at Datchet, superintending the erection of a platform for the new twenty-foot telescope and finishing some of its more delicate parts. Though this new telescope was no longer than the twenty-foot that had been brought from Bath, it was called the large twenty-foot because it had a larger mirror.

William was about to begin his fourth review of the heavens. He was so eager to use this large twenty-foot that he could not wait even for its staging to be completed. During those days Caroline had many a fright. She says: "It seemed as if every moment I was alarmed by a crash or a fall, knowing William to be elevated fifteen or sixteen feet on a temporary crossbeam instead of a safe platform. The ladders did not even have their braces at the bottom, and one night in a very high wind he had hardly touched the ground before the whole apparatus came down. Some neighboring men were called upon to extricate the mirror, which fortunately was uninjured; but much work for the carpenters was cut out for the next day."

After the large twenty-foot telescope was erected Caroline had little time for observing with her own. She says regretfully, "I had marked only fourteen nebulae when my sweeping was interrupted by my being employed to write down my brother's observations."

Every evening as soon as the stars appeared, William and his assistant were ready to begin their night's work. When a special star came into view, William would give its position and whatever description of it he wished recorded. Caroline would note the exact time of its appearance and whatever dictation he gave regarding it. Before writing anything down, however, she would repeat his words aloud so that he could be sure she had heard them and would record them correctly.

The winter nights were very cold. Occasionally William would go inside to warm himself. He would exchange his frosted garments for others that his sister had placed near the fire.

In the morning after breakfast and a few hours of sleep, one might see William's untiring secretary, homemaker, and assistant go into the library, get out the proper record books, and begin copying into them the items noted during the night. She assigned one book to the moon, one to Mars, others to the sun, double stars, and nebulae. Very carefully she transcribed each item into its proper record book, where William could quickly find the desired information regarding any particular object he might have reason to refer to.

When the night's dictation had been recorded, she would attack the pile of letters waiting to be sorted. There were often letters from prominent astronomers in England, France, Germany, and Prussia, congratulating Herschel on one discovery or another. Caroline's heart swelled with pride. William was not only the dearest of brothers, he was the most wonderful!

Sorting the contents of the library shelves, she

might find one of William's scientific papers that must be copied before he sent it to the Royal Society, and she would work on that until her hand was tired.

Perhaps she would run across memoranda listing the parts of a recently finished telescope, with instructions for assembling it. A copy must be made to send the purchaser with his newly acquired instrument. This would receive immediate attention.

As she hurried to the kitchen to supervise preparations for the evening meal, she could look back on a busy day, and half aloud, with a sigh of satisfaction, she would say, "I've done my very best today to help my brother."

The evening candles were lighted; stars appeared one by one; William climbed to his observation platform; she followed with notebook and pencil to her little room under the telescope, where she could hear him through the speaking tube. If the sky was clear and observation good, they might continue their work until the stars faded out in the early dawn. At times during the long winter nights William might observe as many as three or four hundred stars and Caroline would note his observations on many of them.

Soon she would make an important discovery of her own!

Chapter 6

Secrets of the Double Stars

ONCE CAROLINE was gathering some copied sheets and fastening them together. She sighed. "How ignorant I am of all these things that my brother writes about so wisely!"

Caroline had decided that the only way she could get an education was by asking questions and remembering the answers, and she was right. There was no time to sit down for formal lessons. So she improved every opportunity to gather information by the question-and-answer method—mostly at mealtimes, the only spare times they had.

We can imagine listening to them one day at the table.

William is speaking:

"Perhaps you do not understand astronomical theory as well as some of the rest of us, but your work is very valuable to me. You know many things that were unknown to the old Greek philosophers."

"You mean, their thinking that

the earth was flat like a pancake, and not a globe?"

"Well, from Plato's time on (about 400 B.C.) the Greek philosophers agreed that the earth was a globe, but in earlier centuries they thought it was flat, and so might you if all you had to judge by was what you could see from the spot where you were standing. In ancient times it was generally supposed that the earth was the center of the universe, while the sun, moon, and all the stars were traveling around it, as they appear to be doing.

"Even before Plato there were a few men whose thinking was in advance of their time. Pythagoras, a learned Greek scholar who lived and taught before 500 B.C. (or at least some of his followers), declared the earth to be a globe, but still thought that the rising and setting of the sun, planets, and stars were caused by their moving around the earth. About three hundred years after Pythagoras, Heraclides said that their apparent rising and setting were caused by the daily rotation of the earth on its axis.

"About a century later, Aristarchus, a teacher in the University of Alexandria, maintained that the earth traveled around the sun and not the sun around the earth.

"About four hundred years later came Ptolemy. He was one of the greatest of ancient astronomers, yet he rejected the idea that the earth rotated on its axis, and he had strange ideas concerning the arrangement of the planets. He worked out a theory of the motions of the heavens that is very amusing to us today."

"Did these men have proof?" Caroline asked.

"They proved them to their own satisfaction, but

often failed to convince their fellow astronomers. Once in a while a progressive investigator would come close to the truth.

"Not long after Aristarchus lived, there was another astronomer named Eratosthenes, who not only declared that the earth was a globe but actually estimated its circumference."

"How did he do that?" Caroline wanted to know.

"He was in charge of the great library in Alexandria, Egypt, and he learned from one of the books there that on the longest day of the year, at Syene, a town some distance south of Alexandria, up the Nile, the sun was directly overhead at noon. At the city of Alexandria at that same noon it was 7.2° south of overhead. So he divided 360—the number of degrees in a full circle—by 7.2, and that gave him 50. Then he reasoned that if the earth was a sphere, its circumference would be 50 times the distance (about 500 miles) from Alexandria to Syene. This gave him an answer, 24,850 miles."

"How close he came to the truth!" Caroline exclaimed.

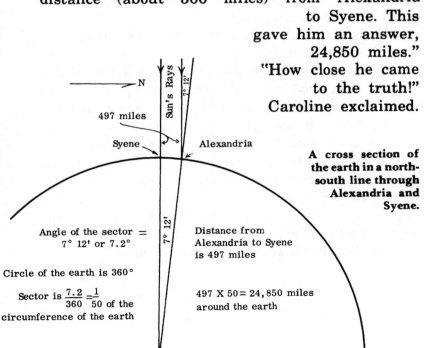

A cross section of the earth in a north-south line through Alexandria and Syene.

497 miles

Sun's Rays

7° 12'

Syene

Alexandria

Angle of the sector = 7° 12' or 7.2°

7° 12'

Distance from Alexandria to Syene is 497 miles

Circle of the earth is 360°

Sector is $\frac{7.2}{360} = \frac{1}{50}$ of the circumference of the earth

497 X 50 = 24,850 miles around the earth

"Yes, indeed, it was a close estimate and a wonderful discovery to be made way back in those days, without the telescope or the many other devices that astronomers now have to aid them in their investigations."

"When did people find out the real facts about the motion of the earth?"

Between bites William went on to say, "About 250 years ago a Polish monk named Copernicus watched the sky for many years, and then wrote a book about what he had learned. He showed plainly that this earth traveled around the sun. He died in 1543."

"Did people read his book and learn the truth?"

"Yes, it was widely read by the schoolmen, and it caused great discussion. Some said, 'Copernicus has proved everything he tells us about the movement of the sun and the planets.' But others said, 'His theory cannot be right, because it doesn't agree with what Aristotle taught.' "

Then very naturally came Caroline's next question, "Who was Aristotle?"

"He was one of the greatest of the Greek philosophers who lived in the fourth century B.C. Like the others of his time, he believed that the earth was a globe, but he thought that the stars traveled around it. Aristotle was such a great scholar that for centuries his teachings were followed without question in all the principal universities of the land. It was regarded as foolish, and even sinful, to doubt anything in his writings. No one had a right to investigate or to experiment or to find out anything different from what Aristotle had taught."

"Then how did anybody ever discover the truth?" persisted the eager questioner.

"They did not find out enough to prove that Copernicus was right until the telescope was invented, which brought them a nearer view of the heavenly bodies."

By now William had finished eating. He rose to go, when another question detained him. "How long ago was that? How long have we had the telescope?"

He was always glad to talk with his sister on anything pertaining to the stars, provided he was not busy at the moment working on some intricate problem or exacting project.

"Would you like to hear the story?" he asked, seating himself again in his chair. "It was in the year 1608, about 175 years ago. A spectacle maker in Holland happened to pick up two lenses and place one in front of the other so he could see through both at the same time. He looked through them at distant objects. The cock on the weather vane on the church steeple appeared life size and quite near. He had found a way to bring distant objects closer and to make them appear larger. News of his discovery spread over Europe.

"A certain mathematics teacher named Galileo heard of it. He took a piece of organ pipe, and fastening a lens at each end, looked through it at distant objects. It brought them nearer and made them brighter. He used his crude instrument to study the moon, and saw dark and bright spots on its surface. The bright star Venus was in the sky at the time. He watched it night after night and noticed that it changed its shape—it showed phases like the moon.

" 'It's true! It's true! Copernicus is right! Venus is revolving around the sun! And if Venus, then the other planets! We are traveling around the sun, and not the sun around us! The proof has come!' Galileo was so excited he nearly dropped the crude instrument he held in his hand. As night after night he continued to watch the heavenly bodies, he saw many other sights that proved Copernicus to be correct. He named the newly invented instrument the *telescope.*"

"Then everybody had to believe the truth," announced Caroline with finality.

"Not everybody." William shook his head. "A few who looked through Galileo's telescope were convinced because they saw the proof. Others said, 'Galileo is deceiving us. The whole thing is magic and Galileo is a wicked wizard.' He was ordered not to teach his theory, and finally was commanded to deny that he himself believed it."

Caroline was indignant: "How absurd! How ridiculously absurd!"

William smiled. "A little more than a century and a half ago Kepler discovered the shape of the path in which a planet travels around the sun. He described it as an ellipse, an elongated circle. But Kepler still regarded the sun as the center of the universe.

"Then came Sir Isaac Newton a century ago. He showed that it is the power of gravity, the same power that draws a falling body toward the earth, that keeps the earth traveling in its path around the sun, and the moon in its path around the earth.

"Since the invention of the telescope, astronomy has become one of the most popular of the sciences taught in our universities. Observatories are being established in many of the large cities of Europe. Thus far the solar system holds the attention of most of our great scientists. Very little is yet known of the stars lying beyond. Before we can explore the distant stars we must have more powerful magnifiers."

"Thanks, William, for taking the time to explain all this to me. Now I understand why you are so greatly interested in making better telescopes."

The history lesson was finished.

During their first year at Datchet, William and Caroline, with occasional help from Alexander, accomplished an unbelievable amount of work. Many were the dangers to which they were exposed, especially at night, as they moved rapidly in and out among machinery and pulleys or climbed about over the staging that supported the telescopes. Caroline told of one experience in which she nearly lost her life.

"New Year's Eve had been cloudy, but about ten o'clock a few stars became visible, and in the greatest hurry all was made ready for observing. My brother, at the front of the twenty-foot telescope, directed me to make some alteration in its motion, which was done by machinery. At each end of the machine was an iron hook such as butchers use to hang joints upon. The ground was covered a foot deep with melting snow, and while running in the darkness, I fell on one of these hooks, which entered my right leg about six inches above the knee.

I heard my brother call, 'Make haste!' but could only answer by a pitiful cry, 'I am hooked!'

"Immediately he and one of the workmen lifted me, but in doing so they left about two ounces of flesh on the hook. The workman's wife was called but was afraid to do anything. I disinfected the wound and tied a handkerchief around it. Word of the accident was sent to Dr. Lind, and he brought ointment and lint and told me how to use them. He said that if a soldier had met with such a hurt, he would have been entitled to six weeks' nursing in a hospital."

Caroline thought little of the wound or the pain. Her thoughts were all for William. She was afraid that the interruption caused by her accident might result in his losing some important view through the telescope. But this was not the case. Immediately after the accident the night again turned cloudy, and for sixteen nights afterward there were only a few short intervals favorable for sweeping. Caroline limped around, trying to help a little here and there, until one evening the clouds cleared away, and William spent the entire starlit night at the telescope, and Caroline was with him.

For years William had been making a special study of double stars, that is, two stars so close together that they usually appear as one to the naked eye. Some of these only seem to be together because they are nearly in the same line of sight; others are actually a pair moving around each other.

When William, in his "review of the heavens," came to such a star that he had viewed before, he would ask Caroline for the record made of it on former sweeps. He would then compare these earlier recordings with his more recent observations. By doing this he could note any change in position or appearance. The slightest change was carefully recorded for future comparison. By noting these changes over a period of years, William learned much about the movements of the heavenly bodies.

He discovered several hundred real pairs of double stars—*binary* stars, they are called. Caroline recorded the position of each on the map of the sky as he reported it to her while making observations.

"Well, here it is, finished at last," she said one day with evident satisfaction as she placed in his hands a catalog she had been working on for months, listing the new double stars he had discovered.

"More than four hundred double and multiple stars thus far," she informed him. "I have made the lists from this record book entitled *Double Stars.* This is the book into which I copied your entries on this particular subject."

William smiled appreciatively: "A splendid piece of work, Lina, and one that has required much patience, I am sure. This study of double stars will richly repay us for the years we have devoted to it. It has revealed important facts that may finally lead to solving the mystery of the skies."

"You said once that some of the double stars listed in the star catalogs were not doubles at all," Caroline ventured.

"Yes, that is true. There are many that look like pairs when seen through the telescope that really have no special attraction for each other. They appear to be doubles merely because they are in the same line of vision, one partly hidden behind the other. But there are real double stars, pairs that seem to be held together by some strong attraction that makes them revolve around each other."

Caroline asked, "How can you be certain that they are double stars, or pairs, and not just in the same line of sight?"

In a true binary system, two stars rotate around each other. When they are beside each other, the telescope shows two. When they are behind each other, there seems to be only one.

"Because they sometimes appear as one star and sometimes as two. First, we see both stars of the pair. Then one slowly disappears behind the other. It is circling the central star and is now hidden behind it. After some time it gradually appears again, but on the opposite side from where we saw it disappear. It is coming out from behind the star which it has been circling, and is slowly coming into view; finally, after a long time—it may be years—we see two stars again."

"This is all very puzzling to me," said Caroline.

William continued, "I am convinced that the mighty force that interacts between these distant suns is the power of gravity, the same power that keeps the planets traveling around the sun."

---

* Scientists do not know the cause of gravity. But if you want to know what the Bible says about the power that holds the heavenly bodies in their paths, read Colossians 1:17 and Hebrews 1:3, and those two chapters.

In awe, she said, "Then it is true that each one of these small points of light is a sun shining with its own light, perhaps giving light to a whole family of worlds, while traveling with them through space. Is this the great fact that the heavens teach us?"

"Why not!" her brother replied. "Why would all other suns be different from our sun? Our sun has planets circling it."

So, night after night, newly discovered wonders kept the two fascinated with the glory, the magnitude, the orderly arrangement, the marshaled movements, of innumerable suns, revealing more and more the vast extent of the universe. Herschel's sweeps of the heavens were constantly bringing into view new marvels that awakened their reverence and awe.

When William turned his twenty-foot toward the Milky Way, he exclaimed in amazement, "I now see thousands of shining orbs where before there were only fields of solid, milky whiteness." In certain areas of the heavens, no more than a quarter the size of the moon, he once counted five hundred stars; and one night he estimated that fifty thousand stars had passed his sight through the telescope in an hour's time.

"In learning of these wonders of the heavens," he said to Caroline, "I believe we are receiving instruction from the great Workmaster of nature."

"Ah, yes, William," she agreed. "And to think that I can have a part with you in this grand work!"

The second year at Datchet was extremely severe. Often the tube of the seven-foot telescope would be coated with ice. Caroline had trouble with her ink freezing in the bottle. In midwinter

William wrote: "Not only my breath freezes on the side of the tube, but more than once I have found my feet fastened to the ground with ice when I have looked long at the same star."

One morning about five o'clock, when for several days the temperature had fallen unusually low, the large mirror in the tube of the twenty-foot telescope cracked as a result of the frost, and there was a loud report like the shot of a gun. Preparing another large mirror for his favorite telescope would mean days, even weeks, of arduous labor. William went cheerfully about the task. No trifling accident should deter him from pressing on toward his goal—the solving of the mystery of the stars.

Three years at Datchet, on the marshy banks of the Thames, brought on repeated attacks of fever. William became seriously ill and went to London to consult Sir William Watson, Senior. The doctor prescribed for him, but something more than medicine was needed.

When William returned home he reported, "The doctor says that we have to find a drier, more healthful location." There was no regret to be seen on Caroline's face. She made no objection this time to making another move. She simply remarked, "I am glad we are going to get out of this cold, dreary, dilapidated, old house. Surely somewhere in this beautiful England we can find a pleasanter, more healthful place to live and work."

Chapter 7

The Giant Telescope

WHAT'S THE BIG project now, Herschel?" Caroline's old friend, Watson, was talking to William. Caroline did not want to be caught eavesdropping, but she was interested. The visits of this particular friend always spread good cheer in the Herschel home.

Watson's question was a shot in the dark, but it brought a ready response from William.

"The project? A forty-foot telescope, Watson."

"Why do you need that? I understand that you already have magnifiers of prodigious powers."

"Yes, but great mysteries still lie beyond their reach. I need an instrument with a wider aperture that will admit more light than any I now have, one equipped with a larger mirror that will reflect a more detailed image. I want to penetrate farther into space and learn of the form and extent of the universe."

"I've heard you say that before, Herschel. I've heard you say that you want to discover the construction of the heavens."

"That's it, Watson! That is the goal toward which I have bent all my efforts ever since I got my first view of the starry expanses through a cheap little rented telescope."

The idea caught Watson's imagination. Back at the resort in Bath, Watson told Madam Schwellenberg, a friend who was visiting there. Madam Schwellenberg talked to Sir Joseph Banks, and Sir Joseph Banks talked to King George III. King George was eager for his countrymen to receive all the honor possible from great scientific discoveries. He immediately appropriated two thousand pounds toward the construction of a forty-foot telescope.

The Herschels had followed the doctor's advice and moved to a more healthful location at Clay Hall, in Old Windsor. Even before they were through with moving and settling, William began drawing plans for the giant telescope. His enthusiasm was shared by Alexander and Caroline. One of the upstairs rooms in the house they were occupying was immediately turned into a forge for shaping tools and metal parts. William was about to order materials for building a foundation for the new telescope when the landlady decided to raise the rent. She was not pleased to have Clay Hall, her quiet home, turned into a manufacturing establishment. She threatened to continue raising the rent with every "improvement" made on the place. William looked around and found another location at Slough (pronounced to rhyme with bough), not far from Clay Hall. Here a brick house stood on a rise of ground,

94

with stables on one side and a large garden at the back, surrounded by rows of majestic elms. "Exactly suited to our needs!" was William's pronouncement. Caroline was delighted.

The telescopes were at once set up, and without interruption the stargazing continued. Caroline wrote: "Amid all the hurrying business of moving, every moment after daylight was allotted to observing. The last night in Clay Hall was spent sweeping till daylight, and by the next evening the telescopes were ready for observing at Slough, and the fourth review of the heavens was begun."

Caroline continued making her recordings. She fell behind with the copying and lost two or three sheets, because for a few days it was impossible to find a place to set up the writing table. Machinery, mirrors, half-finished telescopes, and parts were strewn everywhere.

"In short," she wrote, "the entire place was at one time a manufactory of optical instruments. I had frequent calls to go into the workshops when I was obliged to run to my brother with questions. Usually at such times I found him surrounded by twenty to forty workmen waiting to carry out his orders. A carpenter with his crew was there from town. A blacksmith was at work in the washhouse. In a barn near the house another blacksmith with his workmen was forming a giant iron tube. The sheet from which it was being made measured forty feet in length and fifteen feet four inches in width. Outside the building, men were leveling ground and laying brick for the foundation of the telescope. Others were rooting out trees."

Regretfully Caroline watched the stately elms

"We shall call that building Observatory Cottage, Caroline. It will be your residence, library, and study."

crash, one after another. "Oh, if only we could save these grand old elms!" she cried, "but I know it cannot be. This is the site for our observatory, and nothing must be permitted to shut out the sky."

When she could endure the sight no longer she turned away to watch the carpenters, who were busily transforming the stable into a two-story apartment. She looked up to see William standing by her side. "This is to be your residence," he said. "I think we shall call the large brick building Observatory House, and your domicile Observatory Cottage. The room opening into the garden will make a good library and study. We shall set up the small twenty-foot outside near the door, where it will be handy."

The large twenty-foot was erected in the center of the garden, and smaller telescopes elsewhere in the garden. A Newtonian telescope was erected on a flat portion of the roof of Observatory Cottage for Caroline's exclusive use. Opposite the cottage stood a number of small workshops.

Work on the forty-foot was well under way when there came an interruption in the form of a summons from King George III. The word that William brought back from his interview with the king that day was the cause of some excitement.

"He wants me to deliver a telescope of my own make as a royal gift to the Observatory of Göttingen. I shall have to start as soon as possible, and I would be glad, Alexander, for you to accompany me on the trip. I suggest that you bring your wife to stay here so she can keep Caroline company while we are gone."

Mrs. Herschel came to be with Caroline, and on

the next day, June 3, 1786, the two brothers set off on their errand, stopping at Hanover for a few days on their way. From there William wrote a newsy letter to his sister. The letter brought her a dull sense of loneliness. How she would love to be with her brothers, to see the hometown again, to greet her mother and all the old friends.

"But it's my duty to stay on the job," she announced to her companion. "The workmen must be paid their wages, and someone must keep an eye on the pilferers, to see that they do not run away with all the valuables on the premises."

"What! You mean to say there are thieves on this place!" said Mrs. Herschel.

"Yes, indeed! Almost every day valuable articles vanish. The most regrettable loss is a whole drawerful of data recording William's experiments on rays of light and heat. They were in the drawer of a table that was taken from the laundry room. You see why I cannot leave. I am glad you are here to keep me company."

"And I am glad that I don't have to stay at home alone either."

As soon as the brothers were gone Caroline opened a new record book and called it *Book of Work Done.*

Her first entry was, "By way of not suffering too much from sadness, I began with bustling work. I cleaned all the brasswork for the seven- and the ten-foot telescopes, and put curtains before the shelves to hinder the dust from settling upon them again."

The next day she wrote: "I cleaned and put the polishing room in order, and made the gardener clean the work yard, put everything in safety, and mend the fences." Two days later she told of spending the morning with Mrs. Herschel at needlework, and of taking her to Windsor in the afternoon.

July 6: "I put all the philosophical letters in order, and the collection of each year in a separate cover." A little later she received a visit from Dr. and Mrs. Maskelyne and some of their illustrious friends.

One morning Prince Charles, the queen's brother, and two other members of the royal family came with a request from the king that they be shown the instruments.

She spent the pleasant starlit nights on the roof of Observatory Cottage, continuing her sweeps of the heavens, with Mrs. Herschel at her side taking a peep through the telescope now and then. During the day most of her time was occupied bringing the star catalog up to date and adding William's latest discoveries. She hoped to have it finished, with the 2,500 recordings of recently discovered nebulae, by the time he came home.

On the thirteenth she wrote, "I wound up the sidereal timepiece and Field's and Alexander's clocks, and made covers for the new and old registers."

August 1, almost one month after the brothers had left for Göttingen, she made this entry: "I have calculated 100 nebulae today, and this evening I saw an object which I believe will prove tomorrow night to be a comet."

August 2: "Today I calculated 150 nebulae. It has been raining throughout the whole day, but seems now to be stopping a little." Evidently she waited up that night hoping to get a clear glimpse of the sky, for at one o'clock she wrote: "The object of last night *is* a comet." There is nothing in this simple entry to indicate the excitement she must have felt when she really knew that she had discovered a comet—her first.

The following night was cloudy, and she spent the evening writing letters to her brother's astronomer friends in London, announcing her discovery of the comet and telling them where to look for it in the heavens. Letters of congratulation came in. This new comet was to be called the "Lady's" comet, for Caroline was the first woman to make such a discovery. With satisfaction, Caroline laid these letters aside to show William and Alexander when they returned—a little surprise for them!

August 6 was clear, but Caroline's observations were interrupted by Sir Joseph Banks and Lord Palmerston, who came bringing a friend to look at her comet through her own telescope. The days were now more crowded. Compiling William's catalog of nebulae was a prodigious task and progressed slowly. In the meantime she must not neglect making recordings of her own discoveries. And there were other duties connected with the workshops. She had to hunt up a man to help the blacksmith. Trips must be made to town to pay bills and purchase items in preparation for her brothers' return.

About the middle of August the brothers arrived, and Caroline was glad to turn over the management of the telescope factory to William. She told him, "I've tried to keep all the letters and records in order and the accounts straight; I've entertained scores of stargazers; I've scolded the workmen when they were dilatory and commended them when they did good work; and I've managed to settle most of their quarrels."

"You have done well, little sister," William said. Alexander added, "You are a heroine!" She handed William the correspondence she had carried on with his astronomer friends, men who were now her special friends also. William praised her: "Now that you have discovered a comet yourself, you are more than an astronomer's assistant, you are *an astronomer.*"

Without delay William resumed the construction of the forty-foot telescope. In writing of this, Caroline said, "The following two years were spent in a perfect chaos of business. The garden and workrooms were swarming with laborers and workmen, smiths and carpenters, going to and fro between the forge and the forty-foot machinery. And I ought not to forget that there is not one screw bolt about the whole apparatus but what was fixed under the immediate eye of my brother. I have seen him lie stretched out many an hour in the burning sun, across the top beam while the ironwork for the various motions was being fixed."

At last the great iron tube was finished. The sides had been trimmed and fastened together by seaming, without any rivets. William instructed the workmen to carry the tube to the garden and lay it on a floor of circular blocks that had been built for it. There it was to remain until the gigantic wooden framework in which it would swing was finished. But now came a second interruption in the construction work—William ran out of money. All winter the great tube lay on its temporary platform exposed to the weather. Frosts cracked the

"Come, my Lord Archbishop," said the king from inside the great tube. "I will show you the way to heaven."

rocks supporting it, and cedar timbers had to be inserted between the tube and the rock platform. Sir Joseph petitioned the king for more money.

One day the king, the queen, and the princesses, accompanied by dukes, lords, and ladies, and by the Archbishop of Canterbury—all came to see what progress was being made. Someone in the party suggested that they take a walk through the tube while it lay on the platform. They had to stoop, for the tube was only about five feet in width. His Majesty led the way and the others followed. Noticing that the archbishop was having difficulty, the king turned to give him a hand, saying as he did so, "Come, my Lord Archbishop, I will show you the way to heaven." Caroline brought out the visitors' book and had them write their names under date of August 7, 1787.

One week after the visit, King George gave a second two thousand pounds for work on the telescope. He also put Caroline on a salary of fifty pounds a year as an assistant.

It was not until 1789 that the wooden framework for the forty-foot was complete, and the great iron tube was hoisted into position. William demonstrated the movements of the machinery to the satisfaction of all the onlookers.

Caroline stepped up. "Let me see if I can move it." She took hold of one of the handles. Up went the mammoth tube. Then, lightly, down it came again. "I never thought I would be able to move a monster like that all by myself," she said.

But for observations it took two men to move the tube and turn the whole supporting framework on its circular track (see the title page). Two small rooms were built into the structure that supported the telescope. One was for Caroline to sit in while writing down her brother's observations as he dictated through a speaking tube, and the other was for the men who worked the telescope machinery. William's seat could be moved up and down or sidewise at his pleasure; and there was a gallery across the framework, between the ladders.

The giant telescope was the chief scientific wonder of the age. Slough was crowded with sightseers, many of whom were as greatly interested in the intricate mechanism of the telescope as they were in the objects it revealed.

Before this, however, a great change had taken place in the Herschel household. It must have been one day near the end of 1787 that William came in with an important announcement:

"Mary Pitt has consented to be my wife! Isn't that the best of news!"

It is not surprising that to the prospective bridegroom this seemed the best possible news. Neither is it surprising that to Caroline it should seem quite the contrary, since she was faced with the prospect of being set aside as the mistress of her brother's household.

William was sure that bringing Mary into the family would be a delightful thing for them all. It would comfort Mary, who had been very lonely since her husband's death; and her abilities to make a pleasant home would not only bring her happiness but also relieve Caroline of the household responsibilities that had at times been a tax on her strength.

Now she would have more time for fulfilling her

role as "assistant astronomer to William Herschel." She could be of far greater help to him than when burdened with many household cares. William saw no reason why his sister should not see it that way.

But for Caroline the world had suddenly come to an end. She was about to lose her brother, the one person she adored; the one whose success and happiness had been her very life was about to set her aside for another, so it seemed to her.

Caroline knew Widow Pitt would make William a good wife. She was kindhearted and unselfish, she was cultured and intelligent, and she was rich, as well. Her husband had been a wealthy merchant and had left her generously provided for. Before his death, in 1786, the two families had visited back and forth, and William had spent much time with Mr. Pitt in his library. After Mr. Pitt's death brother and sister had often strolled across the field and through the grove to Upton House, to comfort and cheer Mary in her bereavement.

And now it had come to this! William and Mary were to be married! Caroline's whole life centered in William. She had cared for him, worked for him, lived for him, ever since he had rescued her from her humdrum life in Hanover. For sixteen years every act of her life had been in the interest of her brother, with very little thought for herself.

She had undertaken the shopping, the management of servants, the keeping of accounts, guarding his finances and often skimping herself, in order that William might pay for materials and labor that he needed.

She had relinquished her musical career and accompanied him to London to assist with his astronomical projects. At a time when she was beginning to make her own discoveries, she had left *her* telescope to spend entire nights recording *his* observations as he dictated them to her.

She had cared for his physical needs, standing by his side and putting food into his mouth when he refused to leave his work long enough to sit down to the table. Why had she done all this? Because she loved him, she believed in him, she lived for him. And she had taken for granted that this happy partnership would always continue. Now suddenly she must give up her position of homemaker, companion, and sharer in all his dreams and efforts.

Months passed, while Caroline subdued the resentment in her heart, and William and Mary settled questions regarding their housing arrangements. Naturally Mary preferred to live in her own comfortable and elegant Upton House rather than in the plainer brick house at Slough. But she was sensible enough to know that William had to be near his telescopes and workshops. Finally Mary decided that it would be more pleasant to live at Observatory House than to be separated from William nearly all the time both day and night.

One day early in May, 1788, there was a wedding in Mary's home church. Sir Joseph Banks was best man and, of course, William was the groom. Alexander and Caroline signed the register, after which the little sister presided at the wedding breakfast and then slipped away to her own apartment. Here, no doubt, she shed many a tear. She must have written in her diary some things that nobody but herself ever read, for she destroyed every page referring to this period, probably in later years after she had learned to love the sweet, generous-hearted sister-in-law.

When the first grief was over, Caroline's honest heart told her that Mary Pitt was just the very one William needed to break up his continuous grind of work and bring him some of the pleasures of social life. Mary was gay and lighthearted and fond of entertaining. She insisted that William take a vacation with her at least once a year. They would drive away in their carriage and spend a few weeks at some resort or at the home of friends.

Caroline continued to live at Observatory Cottage, where she was handy to the telescopes. Here on favorable nights she was always ready to take dictation from William, through the speaking tube, from his observation seat sixteen or twenty feet above ground. She found that life went on much as it had before his marriage. In some ways she was better off than before. Relieved now of all household responsibilities, she had more time for her secretarial duties. Then, too, when William and Mary were away from home on their vacation tours, she could have her evenings free for making her own observations and sweeping for nebulae and comets. Yet she treasured the hours that she and William could spend together and would often say, "I am glad, my brother, that you still need my help."

When, four years after her brother's marriage, John Frederick was born, Caroline forgot her sorrows. Cuddling Baby John and carrying him around became Aunt Caroline's chief diversion. As soon as the little fellow could toddle, he would trot down the walk every day to say, "Morning, Aunt Lina"; and she was always happy to see him, although he scattered her papers and interrupted her work with his unending chatter.

For nine years Caroline continued to live in Observatory Cottage, until it became so crowded with books, records, and instruments that she had scarcely room to do her writing. Then she moved successively to several lodgings elsewhere, and in 1803 moved into an apartment at Upton House.

She continued to "mind the heavens" for her brother. On those rare occasions when Mary succeeded in dragging William away from his telescopes for short trips here and there, Caroline would resume the fascinating work of looking into space, sweeping for nebulae and comets with her own Newtonian reflector. During these years she announced the discovery of eight comets, at least five of which had never received notice before.

Among her treasures laid carefully away there was found a small package labeled, "This is what I call 'Bills and Receipts of My Comets.'" The package contained data concerning her discoveries, each folded in a separate paper and marked, "First Comet," "Second Comet," et cetera. She received many letters from prominent astronomers concerning these comets. Some of these letters were given to autograph collectors, but a number have been preserved.

The reports of what could be seen through the giant forty-foot telescope spread far and wide, and it became quite the fashion for amateur stargazers, as well as for renowned astronomers from observatories and universities throughout Europe, to make a trip to Slough. Guests of the royal family visiting Windsor were not expected to leave there until they had taken a look at the sky through this mammoth instrument and had made the acquaintance of its famous inventor and his clever sister.

These distinguished guests were entertained at Observatory House, and on such occasions Caroline was invited to dine with them. Mary presided in the home, but it was Caroline who helped her brother explain the workings of the telescopes. She assisted William in showing their guests whatever wonders were visible in the heavens at the moment, and she saved much of his time by answering their curious questions herself and by diverting them with interesting sights through her own reflector.

Dr. Joseph La Lande, renowned professor of astronomy in the University of Paris, visited the Herschels in their home and became a great admirer of Caroline. One of his nieces was named after her, and the little lady smiled when her attention was called to the numerous crop of Carolines that Europe produced that year. Such delicate compliments pleased her very much.

She worked many months on an index that would enable William and his associates to find the stars listed in Flamsteed's Catalog; and she was greatly surprised when Dr. Maskelyne arranged to have her index published for the use of other astronomers.

Not long after this she received an invitation from Lady Maskelyne to spend a week with the family at Greenwich. Caroline accepted the invitation, because, as she said, it would give her a chance to transfer some corrections that William had made in Flamsteed's observations into Maskelyne's copy. The visit did not prove to be a very restful one. Lady Maskelyne put on so many socials and other entertainments that Caroline had to sit up nights in order to get her copying done.

She was usually too fully occupied with her brother's work to go on pleasure trips. However, she had numerous friends at the royal lodge with whom she spent many pleasant days when William and Mary were absent.

One day at the royal lodge she met a Mrs. Beckedorff, one of the lady attendants on Queen Charlotte. When introduced, she was surprised to hear the lady remark, "Surely you remember me, Caroline, when many years ago we attended Madam Kuster's school of dressmaking in Hanover." Mrs. Beckedorff and her daughter were occupying a private apartment in the lodge. Their renewed acquaintance was a great delight to both Caroline and Mrs. Beckedorff. It continued for years, until the time of Queen Charlotte's death, when her devoted attendant returned to her home in Hanover.

Caroline's brother, Alexander, would often come up from Bath and spend his vacation time working on the telescopes. After being married only a few years, his invalid wife had died. An occasional visit with his cheerful little sister now offered a pleasant interlude in his otherwise lonely existence.

At one time Caroline's rooms were cluttered with the optical apparatus of a twenty-five-foot telescope that was being packed at the barn for shipment to the king of Spain. It was one of the finest instruments of its kind William had ever made. Caroline mourned the years of taxing labor that its construction had cost him, but was somewhat comforted when she learned that he received £3,150 in payment for it.

William and Caroline were honored all over Europe. They had made many important discoveries. Still there were mysteries not yet solved.

Chapter 8

Unsolved Mysteries

"MARY," William Herschel said to his wife one morning, "last night I completed my fourth review of the heavens."

Mary gave her husband one of her radiant smiles. "How glad I am to know that you have at last finished that tremendous task!"

"I began my first review nearly twenty-five years ago. Since then, with one or another of my telescopes, I have made 1,112 sweeps across the sky, scrutinizing and recording, one by one, all the principal stars visible in our northern sky. I have noted the position of each, its color, its degree of brightness, and whether it is single or double. I have examined every object of interest to be seen in our heavens—sun, moon, planets, stars, nebulae, star clusters, comets, satellites, and asteroids, and Caroline has kept a careful record of my observations. Her catalogs and books report all my findings.

112

"When we began our work there were only 150 nebulae or star clusters listed in the printed catalogs. We have added 3,000 more to the lists. If telescopes could be made of higher magnifying powers than those we have used, we should doubtless find thousands more."

Mary was interested in the stars, but she was far more interested in William. She patted his shoulder. "I hope, my dear, that you will not try to discover them all. Surely you have made your contribution to the science of astronomy. Why not leave a million or two stars for your fellow scientists to find, while you take a well-deserved rest? I've been thinking that it is time to make that trip to Paris we have been talking about for months."

After much persuasion Mary managed to get her husband into the stagecoach along with her niece and ten-year-old son, John, and they set off for the French capital. As was to be expected, Caroline declined Mary's invitation to accompany them. Someone must stay to look after things at Observatory House and entertain the visitors.

So Caroline moved over from Upton House and took charge of the central home at Slough while William and Mary were gone.

When William and Mary returned she was interested to hear them tell of their adventures in Paris. William had been granted an audience with Napoleon, and he had found that great man as little interested in astronomy as he himself was in French politics.

At home once more, William was overwhelmed with work as usual. The forty-foot telescope required much care. The mirror weighed more than

2,100 pounds. In order to make it strong enough to be lifted by a crane and lowered into the tube, it had to be made with a large percentage of copper. The copper tarnished quickly, so that the mirror had to be polished frequently. When this was done, the mirror had to be lifted out of the tube and laid on the polishing machine, and a thinner mirror used temporarily. Polishing was no longer done by hand, yet managing the machinery required William's constant oversight.

Caroline fretted as day by day she saw her brother wearing his strength away. She realized the damage that overwork, exposure to cold, loss of sleep, neglect of meals, and now the additional care of the giant telescope, were doing to his health. Anxiety over him began to wear her down.

One night a very bright comet appeared in the sky. Caroline feared that this unusual object would bring a host of sight-seers to Slough to view it through the mammoth telescope. Her fears were no illusion. People flocked to Observatory House. After dismissing his workmen one evening, William was sitting down to eat when a group of fifty or sixty people gathered on the grass plot. The evening was cool; yet without taking time to finish his meal or to put on warmer clothing, he at once went to the telescope and entertained the group until after midnight. The next day he did not feel well. Caroline said, "I believe his nerves received a shock that night from which they never recovered."

During the next several years Herschel was persuaded to take time off from his work to go with his family on tours of North England and Scotland and the South Coast, leaving Caroline in charge at home. Upon returning from these excursions, he would plunge into his work harder than ever. How could he rest when there were so many questions yet unanswered, so many mysteries unsolved? He had hoped the forty-foot telescope would supply the missing answers, but it only added to the mysteries!

Caroline had shared her brother's cherished hope that his new high-powered instrument might reach the limits of the Milky Way and beyond and resolve all the nebulae into stars. But there were sections where no background could ever be seen, only stars, stars, stars—millions of them, gleaming points of light; and one class of nebulae, including the one in Orion's sword, turned out to be, not extremely distant universes, but nearer masses of "shining fluid" of an unknown nature (described by modern astronomers as incandescent gas).

Finally the time came when William had to bid farewell to the forty-foot telescope. His strength was no longer equal to caring for the massive instrument. For the last time he pointed the giant tube toward the great nebula of Orion's sword—the same object to which he had first directed its mirror, even before it was finished, and to which he had returned again and again. Possibly Caroline shared his farewell look at the glory of Orion, though she never made observations through this largest telescope; she was afraid of climbing the ladders.

How much more magnificent the sight appeared through the forty-foot than on the night when they had turned on it that first little 5½-foot Newtonian telescope that William, Alexander, and Caroline had made. Yet through the years no amount of coaxing with the highest-powered lenses in the eyepiece had persuaded even this majestic forty-footer to resolve this nebula into a star cluster. Except for the group of stars within it already known, there was nothing but the same banks and clouds of "shining fluid" in all varying degrees of brilliance.

The heavens teemed with nebulae. The telescope had resolved hundreds into star clusters, star systems composed of millions of shining orbs, like our galaxy, the Milky Way.

If there could be such a thing as a telescope of limitless magnifying power, would it continue throughout all eternity to reveal more and still more star universes, reaching on and on and on, throughout boundless space? This was one of the questions William and Caroline had hoped to solve. But now it seemed to William that life was slipping away before the answer was found. How could he give up? He must live longer! He must work faster!

Caroline was getting old too; her sight was failing and she feared blindness. Troubles were thickening around her. Sophia and Jacob were both dead, and Alexander had had a severe accident and was practically an invalid. Little brother Dietrich was sick, discouraged, and penniless. She took him in and cared for him. Worst of all, William became seriously ill and his life was despaired of.

But after a time the world began to brighten. William rallied. Dietrich recovered and took up his violin teaching again. Caroline's health improved and the threat of blindness was averted. Comforting and cheering others had lifted her own spirits. Her old remedy had worked its magic again.

William's son, John Frederick, was growing

into a strong, brilliant, and handsome young man, which was a never-failing source of joy to his aunt. "He is the pride of the whole family," she would say to her friends. "From the time he entered Cambridge University he has won all the first prizes offered in his classes."

When John finished his schooling Caroline resigned her position at the telescope so that John could take her place at his father's side and catch the inspiration of exploring the heavens.

Under his father's direction John built a twenty-two-foot telescope. This splendid instrument became his favorite, the one he used most often throughout his life.

One morning William and Caroline walked together in the raspberry patch. He was so weak that he leaned on her for support. As they ate the delicious fruit they talked of John's future. William had hoped that this only son of his might enter the ministry; but when John expressed a desire to follow in his father's footsteps and complete if possible the task he had begun, he was satisfied.

Caroline tried to lift her brother's drooping spirits by reminding him of his outstanding achievements. "Dear brother, does it not comfort you to know that you have discovered more of the mysteries of the starry heavens than any other man who has ever lived? You have opened fields of investigation that will keep scientists studying for years to come. You have proved that there is order in the arrangement of the suns and systems that comprise the universe."

"Yes, Caroline, that is all true," William said. "As I have said before, I have looked farther into space than ever a human being did before me, and I have seen stars whose light must have taken two million years to reach the earth."

William was in his eighty-fourth year when Caroline assisted him for the last time copying his papers. His strength had been ebbing for some time, but his death came with unexpected suddenness. As Caroline saw her "best and dearest brother" laid peacefully to rest in the little graveyard beside the church at Upton, her heart throbbed out the cry, "Why could he not have been spared to finish his great and glorious task! So gladly would I have taken his place in death!" Mary grasped Caroline's hand and drew her close. "His was a noble work," she whispered. "As he himself said, by making the wonders of the heavens known to men, he truly glorified his Creator!"

After William's death, John and Mary invited Caroline to live with them, but she said, "No, Dietrich has had a deal of trouble and needs me. He's coming to get me next week; I cannot disappoint him."

Caroline spent the next few days visiting acquaintances in London. Finally Princess Sophia sent her carriage to take her friend to the wharf to board the ship.

Arriving in Hanover, Caroline found Dietrich's family living in an apartment. They had taken an additional room especially for her.

"This is a pleasant room, better than I had expected," she said, as the wife helped her lay aside her wraps and untie her parcels. "I shall be comfortable here. There's ample room for all my books and catalogs and manuscripts.

"My telescope can stand in that corner of the room, but I fear it will be of little service. We are so shut in by buildings that I shall not get a glimpse of the sky."

Callers were refused admittance until Caroline had had a day or two to rest from her journey. Mrs. Beckedorff called, and Caroline was overjoyed to see her old friend. When she returned the call, the lady brought her ten grandchildren and stood them up in a row in the order of their ages. They had been told that they were to meet the wonderful Aunt Caroline, the "lady astronomer" from England, and they were very disappointed when they were presented to a plain little old lady. After the shock of that first meeting, however, they became greatly attached to Caroline and never tired of listening to her stories about the queen and the princesses, and about the big telescope and what she had seen through it.

As news of her arrival spread through the town, old acquaintances flocked to the house, bringing their children and grandchildren.

Among her new acquaintances was Anna Knipping, her niece, one of Dietrich's older girls who still lived in Hanover. She had recently been left a widow with nine children, the youngest still a baby. Anna found a warm niche in Caroline's heart, and became greatly attached to her aunt, who was so attentive to their comfort and so forgetful of her own.

In spite of the many attentions paid her by old friends and by leading citizens of the town, Caroline was lonely. She did not find anyone who cared much about astronomy or was interested in her brother and his discoveries. The people who dropped in to visit the family had few topics of conversation beyond the everyday happenings in the neighborhood. The men would sit around for hours gossiping and smoking and passing remarks on the news, politics, wars, business, and sometimes, for lack of other topics, the weather. Table talk centered around the food, for which, she said, "I care not a pin."

Sometimes there were spirited discussions with Dietrich as to the comparative value of the telescope and the microscope. Caroline had lived so long in contemplation of the starry heavens that it was hard for her to understand why the study of insects was so much more absorbing to her brother than the study of the stars. Once she remarked, "Whenever he catches a fly with a leg more than usual he says it is as good as catching a comet."

But what troubled her more than anything else was Dietrich's unhappiness. He had much to say about his troubles and the unfair deal the world had given him. Caroline was continually reminding him of his many blessings. He had a charming wife and beautiful family; his physical needs were well provided for; but still he looked on the dark side of every cloud.

"Little Dietrich," the infant prodigy, the bright, handsome child, who had been petted and spoiled because of his winsome ways, had turned out to be a near-failure, while the plain, neglected sister who was looked down upon by the family and made the kitchen drudge had, by her unselfishness and constant efforts to brighten the lives of those around her, made her own life beautiful. The lesson early learned that the secret of happiness is not in pursuing happiness for one's self but for others, had crowned her days with glory.

For days Caroline lay weak and exhausted on her couch, trying to brighten the weary hours by recalling pleasant experiences of the past. Her strength returned slowly, and with it the old-time desire to do something to help somebody.

"There must be something I can do that will help John in his work. What can it be?" she kept asking herself. She gathered up the record books and the notes that she had made during the years. "These will save my nephew much time in locating the objects he wishes to observe, and also in making up his catalogs," she mused. Wrapping these packages for shipping kept her busy for several days. But the question persisted, "Isn't there something more that I can do for my nephew?"

She remembered a comprehensive catalog of nebulae and star clusters that she had started for her brother and had worked on for several years. She had brought this unfinished piece of work with her from England, also all of William's *books of sweeps,* in eight volumes, and the numerous notations she had copied regarding them. It made quite a collection. She started work. Now that she had plenty of time she would make a fresh catalog, arranging all the nebulae and star clusters in zones from the North Pole southward. This task fully occupied her time for three years. While she was engaged in it John came over from England. He was astonished to see what a tremendous piece of work she had undertaken, all especially for his personal convenience. He marveled at the devotion to science of his seventy-four-year-old aunt.

Caroline made the catalog with one thought only, that of helping John. Yet it proved so useful to astronomers in general that it won for her the gold medal award of the Royal Astronomical Society of England.

Although not present in person at the presentation, Caroline was praised warmly by the speaker of the occasion. After recounting the extraordinary achievements of her brother William, he said: "Who was it that shared his toils and privations? His sister, Caroline Lucretia Herschel! It was she who by night acted as his secretary; she it was whose pen conveyed to paper his observations as they issued from his lips; she it was who noted the right ascension and polar distances of the objects observed; she it was who, having passed the night near the instrument, took the rough manuscript to her cottage at the dawn of day and produced a fair copy of the night's work; she it was who reduced every observation, made every calculation; she it was who arranged everything in systematic order; and she it was who helped him to obtain his imperishable name."

John lived with his mother in Observatory House until her death. Then, one day he said to his young wife, Margaret, "If I am to carry out my long-cherished ambition to catalog the stars in the southern sky as my father cataloged the stars in the northern sky, we shall have to spend four or five years in South Africa. I want to take you and the children with me. But before we start I must visit Aunt Caroline. She is eighty-two and may not be here when we return."

While on his visit to his aunt in Hanover, John

wrote Margaret: "I found my aunt wonderfully well and very nicely and comfortably lodged; and we have since been on the full trot. She runs about the town with me and skips up her two flights of stairs as light and fresh as some folks I could name who are not a fourth part her age."

John took with him to Cape Town his astronomical records and charts and his favorite telescope, the twenty-two-foot that he had made under his father's direction. Aunt Caroline was as proud as ever of her distinguished nephew and took a lively interest in all his achievements. They often discussed astronomical questions by correspondence. In one of his letters he wrote, "I will try to entertain you with celestial affairs, in which it is delightful to find you taking so much interest." Then he wrote her an account of a magnificent view he had obtained of Saturn with a newly polished mirror.

On his return from the Cape, John again visited his aunt, taking with him his son, Willie, a lad of six.

Caroline was now living alone with an attendant in an apartment. Many honors were showered on the little old lady in her retirement. Princes and princesses sought her out whenever they caught sight of her at public functions, and the king himself often made it a point to have a few words with her. Noted scientists visiting Hanover would invariably stop to make a call on the famous Caroline Herschel before leaving the city. She laughed off their profuse compliments as exaggerations, and was highly amused when people stooped to kiss her hand. Leading citizens brought flowers.

At the age of eighty-eight she was made a mem-

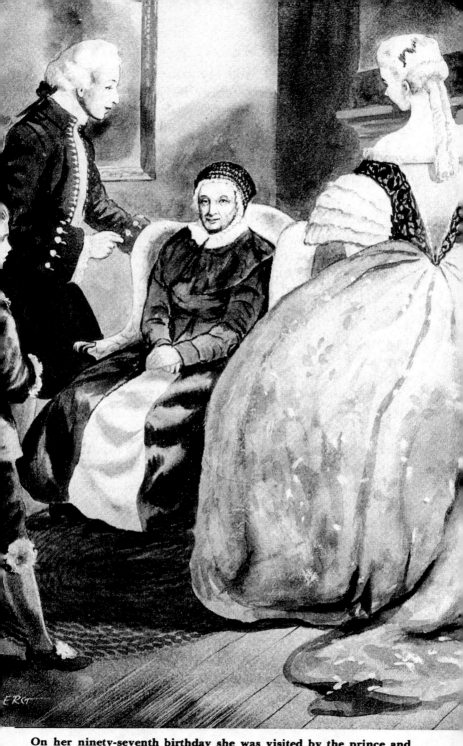

On her ninety-seventh birthday she was visited by the prince and
princess and the small crown prin.

ber of the Royal Irish Academy. For some years she had been an honorary member of the Astronomical Society of England. Yet all the honors shown her by the outside world brought her not one half the pleasure that she took in her nephew and niece and their ten children.

She never met John's wife, nor any of his children except Willie, yet she loved each one, and carried on a delightful correspondence with the family.

One day she sat down to write the story of her life as best she could remember it. She sent it to John's family, for she wanted the children to know the struggles through which Grandfather Herschel had passed on his way up from an obscure oboe player to a world-renowned astronomer. She wrote the stories, one by one, as they came into her mind, and sent them by letter. They were read and re-read by the family; and after Aunt Caroline's death Margaret gathered them up with her diary notes and published them in a book. She called the book *Memoir and Correspondence of Caroline Herschel*. Without this book the account here given of Caroline's life would be much briefer than it is.

On her ninety-third birthday the crown prince and princess paid her a visit, bringing an immense bouquet. Three years later she was awarded the Gold Medal for Science by the king of Prussia. The medal was accompanied by this citation: "In recognition of the valuable services rendered to astronomy by you as a fellow worker of your immortal brother, Sir William Herschel."

She repeated the king's words in a letter to John and Margaret. This was the last letter she ever wrote with her own hand. When her fingers could no longer hold a pen, Miss Beckedorff, the daughter of her old friend, sent monthly newsletters back to England.

On Caroline's ninety-seventh birthday Anna Knipping dropped in to wish her many happy returns of the day. Passing her aunt's door, she saw that there were guests—the prince and princess and the small crown prince. Aunt Caroline was being seated in a beautiful velvet armchair, the gift of her royal friends. She was daintily dressed in a new gown and a new lace cap that Betty, her attendant, had made for her. For two hours she chatted with her guests, doing most of the talking herself, and singing for their entertainment one of William's compositions.

Nine years after John's return to England from South Africa, he published his book *Cape Observations*. It was received with wide acclaim, and at once placed him in the forefront of the scientists of his day. One of the first things he did, of course, was to send a copy to his aunt. As she held the book in her trembling hand she tried to picture William's delight had he lived to look upon this volume in which his own son had recorded the completion of his father's survey of the heavens.

As she neared her ninety-ninth year she became weaker and less active, and spent much of her time reclining on her couch. At four o'clock in the afternoon of January 9, 1848, guns announced the birth of a young prince. When told that this event had taken place, an event to which she had eagerly looked forward, she opened her eyes and smiled. At eleven o'clock she closed them again, and with the smile still on her lips, fell into her final sleep.

To the last she kept alive in her heart the confident hope that she would once again stand by her brother's side, and that, with a closer view of the regions of light and glory than any they had glimpsed through the telescope, they might reach his life's objective and discover the construction of the heavens.

Royal carriages escorted friends and relatives to the garrison church, where burial services were held. After that the coffin was gently lowered into a grave beside that of Caroline's father and mother, and covered with wreaths of laurel and cypress sent by the crown princess.

Around the world flashed the word that Caroline Herschel, the famous lady astronomer, was dead.

But the stars she studied shine on, reminding us of her noble life. And may we not hope that someday you and I, with her, may have a closer view of those distant, radiant orbs which now appear to us only as tiny points of light.

About the Story

The incidents in this story of Caroline Herschel have been collected from the best sources available. Conversation is of course reconstructed, but where it is not derived from letters or journals, it is based on recorded incidents or well-known facts. Personal sentiments attributed to Caroline are not from her pen, for she wrote very little regarding her own feelings. They are from statements of her contemporaries as they knew her, and from her own accounts of her activities as she recorded them in her daybook, her letters, and other writings.

In some instances various accounts recorded by William and his sister or their friends have been combined and abbreviated in an effort to avoid tedious repetition and to make smoother reading. For accurate quotations from the brother and sister it is suggested that you go to the following books:

Memoir and Correspondence of Caroline Herschel, by Mrs. John Herschel (William's daughter-in-law). *The Herschel Chronicle,* by Constance Ann Lubbock (William's granddaughter).

Other books of special interest are:

William Herschel, Explorer of the Heavens, by J. B. Sidgwick.

William Herschel and His Work, by James Sime.

Sir William Herschel, His Life and Works, by Edward S. Holden.

The Herschels and Modern Astronomy, by Agnes M. Clerke.

Herschel, by Hector Macpherson (in the series Pioneers of Progress: Men of Science).

Pioneer Women, fourth series by Margaret E. Tabor.

I Had a Sister, by Helen Ashton and Katharine Davies.

Stories of the Great Astronomers, by Edward S. Holden.

We'd love to have you download our catalog of titles we publish at:

www.TEACHServices.com

or write or email us your thoughts, reactions, or criticism about this or any other book we publish at:

TEACH Services, Inc.
254 Donovan Road
Brushton, NY 12916

info@TEACHServices.com

or you may call us at:

518/358-3494